TOM SHIELDS GOES FORTH

TOM SHIELDS GOES FORTH

TOM SHIELDS

MAINSTREAM
PUBLISHING

EDINBURGH AND LONDON

First published in Great Britain in 2000 by
MAINSTREAM PUBLISHING COMPANY (EDINBURGH) LTD
7 Albany Street
Edinburgh EH1 3UG

ISBN 1 84018 392 6

A catalogue record for this book is available from the British Library

Typeset in Berkeley Book and Opti Civet

Printed and bound in Great Britain by
Butler and Tanner Ltd, Frome and London

CONTENTS

FOREWORD

DESPITE THIS BEING THE AGE of instant electronic communication which enables stories and anecdotes to whizz round the world instantly (and whizz and whizz and whizz around until we are all heartily tired of them), there was still a demand from readers to have yet another collection of items from the *Glasgow Herald* Diary put into print.

Some people appear to have a desire to buy the book as a present for other people, who would rather have received in their Christmas stocking something much more interesting or useful. So, hard luck to those who really wanted a bottle of Remy Martin VSOP, or a box of Cohiba cigars. Anyone who got a bottle of Remy Martin VSOP or a box of Cohibas and actually wanted a copy of this book, please get in touch and a trade can be organised.

If you cannot fathom the raison d'être of this slim volume, think of it as a kind of *Reader's Digest* in reverse – a lot of wee stories with an occasional longer article. Our thanks go to all the *Herald* Diary readers, who did most of the work.

The book is dedicated to the hundreds of former colleagues who have been cast to the winds by the reorganisation and relocation of the *Herald*. People such as the girls in the *Herald* canteen, in the old Albion Street offices. For years they served me food just like my

 **TOM SHIELDS GOES FORTH**

granny used to make. Yes, my granny Maggie McGuigan, God bless her, was a rotten cook as well.

Particular thanks go to Cathie of the canteen night shift for her cheery conversations on the subject of Sydney Devine, the noted Scottish *siffleur* and balladeer. Contrary to received opinion, Cathie was not the lady who threw a pair of substantial knickers at Sydney on the stage of the Pavilion Theatre one evening, leading him to think that the emergency fire curtain had been brought down. Cathie is a big girl, and caused a stir the night of a special Hawaiian promotion in the canteen by wearing a grass skirt. The effect was only marginally diminished by the fact that she wore the grass skirt on top of her overall. Cathie's enthusiasm for the Hawaiian menu on offer was not shared by a chap from the *Herald* print room. Despite her sales pitch, he declined to sample any of the Polynesian delicacies on offer and ordered his usual pie and chips. Detecting Cathie's disappointment, he relented and said: 'On you go. Put a pineapple chunk on the pie.'

TOM SHIELDS
OCTOBER 2000

AND ALONG CAME SMITH . . .

In January 1999, after years of ploughing a lone furrow on the *Glasgow Herald* Diary, Tom Shields was joined in the daily darg by Ken Smith. His addition to the Diary team was warmly welcomed by a reader who commented: 'Oh no, there's two of them now . . .'

Any compliments and kind words about the content of this book should be addressed to Ken Smith. Complaints, as usual, to Tom Shields. Ian Black, Robin Black, Graham Shields, and many others deserve credit.

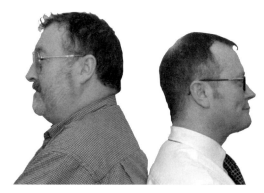

Tom Shields   Ken Smith

1. GONNY READ THIS BOOK

A vignette of a Glasgow couple on the beach in Mallorca. The husband shouts to the wife: 'Gie's ower the suntan lotion.' The wife, perturbed at this peremptory demand, replies: 'Huv you never heard of the word gonny?'

An Ontario linguistics professor told his class: 'In English, a double negative forms a positive. In some languages, though, such as Russian, a double negative is still a negative. However, there is no language wherein a double positive can form a negative.'

To which a Scottish voice piped up from the back: 'Aye, right.'

A TV evangelist is showing off his dog to his pal. 'Can it do tricks?' his pal asks.

'Yes, indeed,' says the evangelist who shouts at his dog: 'Heel!'

'That's not much of a trick,' says his friend, but the evangelist tells his mate to be patient and watch. At that the dog goes over to the pal, puts its paws on top of his head, and closes its eyes in concentration.

An elderly Glasgow woman is very nervous about taking her first flight, and her family have asked the cabin crew to look out for her. A stewardess takes her on board, assures her everything will be all right, and

kindly gives her a cup of tea. She then points to the call button above the old lady's head and says: 'If you would like another cup just press that.'

Shortly after take-off, the crew hear the call button pinging over and over again. Fearing the old lady is in distress, the stewardess rushes down the aisle – to find the elderly passenger holding the cup under the button and pressing it.

Safeway are experts at using elevated language to describe rather simple tasks. A reader tells us his daughter got a job in a Safeway store in the Inventory Management department. Her job involves checking stock and reducing the prices of items near their sell-by date. Or, as one of her colleagues described the post: 'The person with a price gun who walks around the store followed by a queue of loonies looking for bargains.'

Ronnie Simpson of Lismor Records tells us there was a lot of excitement about the Black Watch pipe band's album *Ladies From Hell* receiving a huge number of hits on the traditional music website scottish-irish.com. What was disappointing, though, was that despite the large number of inquiries, very few of the folk checking it out were actually ordering the album. Sadly, when this was looked into by the website masters, they discovered that almost all of the surfers had been searching for the two key words 'black' and 'ladies'. Somehow the rugged chaps of the Black Watch, despite being in kilts, were not quite what they had in mind.

A shopping centre emergency exit had a sign saying: 'Door Alarmed'. Someone had written next to it: 'Window frightened too'.

Two lads from Lothian, Dylan and Jim, are employed by a commercial cleaning firm to tart up offices in the small

honour. He tells of the time he was appearing in a London play and had to go to Glasgow for the initiation ceremony. 'I told the producer that I was going to Glasgow for my rectorial installation. She turned and said to me: "Is there not a hospital here in London that can do that for you?"'

A nun is leading a party of pupils from a Roman Catholic school around Glasgow Cathedral. She points out many interesting and relevant historical bits, including the change of ownership of the premises at the time of the Reformation. She concludes the visit with the words: 'Now let us all kneel down and pray that we get it back.'

N otice in an Irish supermarket: 'Buy one, pay for two, and get the third one free.'

A coffee party (that's the collective noun) of Pollokshields ladies were discussing where they would like their ashes to be scattered. One of the chosen locations was the returns department of Marks & Spencer, where the lady in question said she had spent much of her life.

hours, when they are closed. Their latest contract takes them through to Glasgow where they park their car in what is known as the red-light district, and we're not talking about traffic lights.

Two police officers come up and enquire about what they are doing there, and ask for their names. Something suddenly dawns on Dylan, and with a sigh he tells the officers: 'You might as well arrest us. I'm Dylan Thomas and this is James Bond.' Fortunately, their identities did check out and they were allowed to go about their lawful business.

A ctor Richard Wilson regards his three years as rector of Glasgow University as a great

A chain letter, passed on for fear of suffering bad luck:
'This chain letter was started in the hope of bringing relief to other tired and discouraged women. Unlike most chain letters, this one does not cost anything.

'Just send a copy of this letter to five of your friends who are equally tired and discontented. Then bundle up your husband or boyfriend and send him to the woman whose name appears at the top of the list. Add your name to the bottom of the list.

'When your turn comes, you will receive 15, 625 men. One of them is bound to be better than the one you already have. At the time of writing this letter, a friend of mine has already received 184 men, four of whom were worth keeping.

'An unmarried Jewish woman living with her widowed mother was able to choose between an orthodontist and a successful gynaecologist. You can be lucky too, but do not break the chain. One woman broke the chain and got her own husband back again.'

The two accused in the Lockerbie case were wearing traditional long-flowing Arab dress when they appeared in court on the first day of the trial. A Scots journalist was bemused to hear an American scribe ask court officials: 'Is that what prisoners normally wear in Scotland?'

Word reaches us of delinquency among the female scholars at a certain secondary school in Ayrshire. The wee besoms were beginning to use lipstick and would gather in the school toilets for the application of said devilish make-up. Of more concern to the jannie was that after the Lolitas had put on their lipstick they would press their lips to the mirror, leaving dozens of little prints.

The heidie decided that something had to be done. He called the girls to the bathroom and met them there with the jannie. He explained that all these lip prints were causing a major problem for this poor soul, who had to clean the mirrors every night.

At this point, the jannie gave a demonstration of how he cleaned the mirrors. The good man took out a long-handled squeegee, dipped it into a WC, and then cleaned the mirror. Since then the practice of planting lipstick kisses on the mirrors has been in decline.

patients over the next three years. The first trial will be led by Dr Willy Notcutt at the pain relief clinic at James Paget Hospital, in Great Yarmouth, Norfolk.

Due to the sad inevitability of men frequently dying younger than women, the female residents of a Renfrewshire nursing home are particularly keen when there is a new man who comes to stay. A fresh face has indeed arrived at the home, and one of the women is eager to find out all about him, where he is from, and what he did. Eventually, the chap admits that he has recently been released from prison. But she does not give up, and eventually gets him to admit what he was inside for. Reluctantly he tells her: 'I murdered my wife with an axe.' After digesting this news, she says to him: 'So you're single then?'

The following notice spotted in Gairloch is an example of Gaelic thinking: 'Poolewe Hall Dance. The dance advertised in the *Gairloch Times* for July the 23rd should have been cancelled as it was held the previous week. There is no dance in the Poolewe Hall on Friday, 23 July. Sorry for the disappointment and any inconvenience – Poolewe Hall Committee.'

In a fit of political correctness gone mad, a Kilmarnock school PE teacher renamed the Gay Gordons as the Happy Gordons to avoid blushes among the weans practising for the Christmas dance. There was no word that the pupils were also being taught the Dashing Multi-Racial Sergeant.

It just gets harder and harder for smokers. Normally they are told to take their filthy weed outdoors for a drag, but guests at a dinner in Edinburgh were told on their invitations that 'smoking is permitted only in the stratosphere'. Nocotine junkies contemplating hiring a space shuttle were reassured that as the ceremony is taking place in the Dynamic Earth exhibition in Edinburgh, the stratosphere is, in fact, a side room.

A handy hint on how to deal with those unwanted phone calls from salespersons of windows, conservatories, et al. Bill Waddell of Cumbernauld passes on details of the technique used by his pal Packy (Irish, not Pakistani).

A lady phones Packy keen to sell him a fitted kitchen. 'You sound very young,' says Packy.

'I'm actually 25,' replies the girl.

'So, how do we go about this?' Packy asks.

'I can come along to your house to take measurements tonight, if that's suitable,' replies the saleslady.

'What time?' asks our fella.

'About 6:30,' she says.

'Could you make it 7:30? The wife is going out and we'll have the place to ourselves.' There was an instant and abrupt click as the phone was hung up.

Other suggestions were forthcoming as to how to deal with salespeople phoning you unbidden at home:

If it is a loan they are offering, tell them delightedly how much you could use the money following your bankruptcy.

If BT calls trying to sign you up for Friends and Family, say in a slow voice: 'I don't have any friends. Would you like to be my friend?'

Tell them you don't want double-glazing but ask if, by any chance, they know of a cleaning company that can remove goat's blood stains from carpets.

Regretfully tell them that you work for the same company as they do, and unfortunately they can't sell to a fellow employee.

Say you are busy just now, but add that if they give you their home phone number you will phone them later. When they reply that they don't give out their home numbers, say: 'Is that because you don't want to be bothered by calls from strangers? Well, me neither,' and hang up.

Insist the caller is your mate Des playing a joke and keep on repeating: 'Come on, Des, I know it's you.'

And if they ask how you are, go into great detail about your hernia operation.

Great prizes of our time. Lots at a charity auction at Perth Agricultural Centre included a week in a heated wooden wigwam in Tyndrum, 20 bags of horse manure, and corporate hospitality at a Montrose FC game.

We are told of an American girl who visited the national war memorial chapel at Edinburgh Castle looking for information on her grandfather, who was killed fighting with the Black Watch. A helpful official asked her which war he was killed in, only to be told: 'I don't know. He fought in both.'

A newly divorced chap in Glasgow is trying his first solo supermarket trip. At the deli counter of a Maryhill emporium, he asks the young woman for two ounces of corned beef. This is silently handed over. He then asks for two ounces of gammon. Again she goes about her task, but with a certain lack of enthusiasm. Finally, he asks for a single slice of the cooked ham with egg roll. As the three little packages are slid across the counter she asks: 'Any spare invites for the party?'

 **TOM SHIELDS GOES FORTH** 17

ourts can be confusing places. Take Campbeltown Sheriff Court, where an invalid lady is charged with allowing her dog, Ben, to take a couple of bites out of a paramedic. Her lawyer, John McTaggart, is pleading for the dog not be put down as he is the lady's treasured companion. Trying to be as sympathetic as possible, Sheriff Bill Dunlop asks if Ben's natural aggression could be curbed by castration, and continues the case so that the vet's opinion on the matter could be ascertained.

Lawyer McTaggart is attempting to explain to his client that castration is being considered as a cure for Ben's wayward biting. But she looks perplexed, and loudly asks: 'But how's the dug gonnae be able tae eat wi' nae teeth?'

A lengthy and detailed lonely hearts advertisement appeared in the personal columns of the *John O'Groats News*. It is from an 'attractive Wick divorcee', who is 'starved of suitable masculine company and seeking affection'. She seeks 'the companionship of a virile unattached gentleman with no encumbrances . . . he must be a non-smoker, a moderate drinker, aged between 47 and 62 years, and have a good sense of humour, and a kind, loving and generous nature'.

All pretty straightforward and normal, as far as requests in such columns go. Then the lady gets down to details: 'He can be chunky and cuddly but not overweight with a beer belly or obese. He can be a policeman, or any uniformed occupation preferably.

'He must dress in a masculine, sexy and conventional manner, with a proper short haircut. Height 5ft 7in to 6ft plus. Polite, well-mannered, with a pleasant speaking voice; personally hygienic with clean polished shoes (not tatty trainers).'

Mr Right can look forward to country walks, visits to places of historical interest, Scottish/Irish folk songs in 'old world pubs and taverns', some Country and Western, seaside strolls, and romantic evenings.

There is one final requirement: 'Must be circumcised.'

We are assured there was a caller to directory inquiries who asked for a knitwear company in Woven. The operator replied: 'Woven? Are you sure?'

'Well,' said the caller, 'that's what it says on the label – "Woven in Scotland".'

3 Marriages

SHEPHERD – WOOLLEN

At Watford registry office, on May 13, 2000, Roderick Campbell, second son of the late Mr D.J. Shepherd and Mrs Louisa Shepherd, Rosemount, Dufftown, to Kay Helen, elder daughter of the late Dr. John Woollen and Mrs Mary Woollen, Merry Hill Cottage, Bushey, Hertfordshire.

A story about Auldtimer's Disease, or forgetfulness as it is also called. It involves Wullie who is just back from his holidays. He pops into his local pub, where an acquaintance asks where he has been. Wullie cannot remember.

'It's on the tip of my tongue. Whit's it called again?' Eventually he says to the fellow: 'Whit's that green stuff that grows up the front o' hooses, yon climbin' thing?'

'Ivy?' is the reply.

'Aye, that's right,' says Wullie before turning to his wife and saying: 'Ivy, where did we go oan oor hoalidays?'

You will have heard of the Lincoln-Kennedy conspiracy, the list of coincidences between the assassinations of the two US presidents: both were succeeded by southerners called Johnson. Lincoln was shot at the Kennedy Theater and Kennedy was shot in a Lincoln. But a new one to us is that a week before Lincoln was shot he was in Monroe, Maryland. A week before Kennedy was shot he was in Monroe, Marilyn.

If you read this story often enough, it might eventually make sense. There is this butcher who is famous for the quality of his black puddings. In fact, he has a poster in his window which states: 'Our black puddings are noted.' One day his apprentice is left in charge and a customer asks what the black puddings are noted for. The callow youth ponders before replying: 'They're noted tae keep the juice fae oozin' oot.'

We are told of a teacher in Kilwinning making a home visit to a pupil's abode which, although the family were

friendly enough, seemed to be lacking a bit in the cleanliness department. When the mother offered a cup of tea, the teacher was reluctant to accept but was eventually persuaded. As she sipped from the large mug which was offered to her, she noticed the family Alsatian developing a great interest in her, and sticking its drooling muzzle on her neat Marks & Spencer skirt. At which point the wean shouted: 'You've gi'en the teacher the dug's mug!' No, we don't know why the dog had a mug. We can only assume it's a Kilwinning thing.

A reader staying at the Hamilton Hotel in Seoul, Korea, is still puzzling over the statement in the guest information book in his room which told him: 'Hotel is not responsible for the interaction of ugly morals between guests and employees.'

There is an East/West divide in Glasgow. A lady in the West End had a business removing body hair. Clients telephoning for an appointment would invariably say 'upper lip', 'under arms', or 'bikini line, please'.

When she moved to the East End, the requests were for 'tache', 'oaxters', or something else which we couldn't mention in a family newspaper.

A discussion between a referee and a player who has just been yellow-carded for foul play. The miscreant did not accept his punishment with good grace.

'What would you do,' the malefactor asked, 'if I called you a bastard?'

'You would get the red card,' was the reply from the hard-pressed and underpaid referee.

The footballer continued: 'What if I only thought you were a bastard?'

'I couldn't do anything about that.'

'I wouldn't get a red card then?'

'No.'

'Well, I think you're a bastard,' the player said.

2. EMILY, SARAH, CHELSEA AND KELLY-MARIE

A possibly apocryphal tale of an English chap who had to spend some days and nights in Larkhall on business. His early evening repose was constantly interrupted by snatches of music. On inquiring, he was told that the tunes were respectively 'The Sash', 'Old Derry's Walls', and 'The Green Grassy Slopes of the Boyne'. They were lovely tunes, but why was he hearing from the distance only brief renditions of them? 'I'm sorry,' his host said, 'we have no control over the ice cream vans.'

A tale of progressive parents who had put much effort into improving their four-year-old son's vocabulary. They sought to rid the boy of such childish expressions as choo-choos, doggies, moo-cows, din-dins, pee-pees, and the like. Hard work it was, but rewarding. One evening after the wean had gone to bed, Mummy called up to see if he was asleep yet. 'No,' came the answer, 'I'm still reading Winnie the Shite.'

It is a complex job being an educational psychologist, what with the immense societal pressures school weans are

THE TECHNOLOGICALLY ADVANCED,
BONK-PREVENTING SPORTS DRINK

under these days. But one professional in this field has simplified the whole process somewhat: 'You can be pretty sure that the pupil's name will be a reliable guide to the problem. If she's called Emily or Sarah she will be suffering from an eating disorder. If she's called Chelsea or Kelly-Marie she's being shagged by her uncle.'

We asked Ian MacLeod, manager of the Park Bar, well-known haunt of highland and island folk in Glasgow, to fax us details of an event. He said he couldn't because his fax machine was out of paper. Sometimes we think he sits up all night writing these teuchter one-liners.

The *Irish Times* carried a summary of the policies of Mary McAleese, a contender in the Irish presidential race. Ms McAleese is very much to the point, especially on the subject of family planning: 'I don't want to ram the rhythm method down people's throats.'

There is ongoing debate about whether Scotland should have independence on the Internet and be free of the tyrannical yoke of that .uk bit at the end of addresses. The British Standards Institute, which rules on these matters, is apparently in two minds on the matter. One opinion is Scotland would need to be totally independent before

a new .ending could be awarded. Another school of thought on the BSI Internet committee is that Caledonia can be devolved on the information superhighway. (Or the information single-track road with which we are still lumbered here on the Diary.)

There is also debate as to what an appropriate Scottish ending might be. Most of the obvious choices have already been snapped up, such as .sc by the Seychelles and .ec by Ecuador. Even .cu (as in Jimmy), suggested by an astute reader of *Computer Weekly*, already belongs to Cuba.

Is .mac already spoken for? Will the hamburger chain complain?

M any moons ago in the Diary, we delved into uncomplimentary descriptions of the human face. Pat Donnelly of Glasgow wrote then that the face which adorned the Diary itself was 'like a werewolf peerin' ower a dyke'. Mr Donnelly has since been back in touch: 'May I now say that the current version of your physiognomy which removes your chin and forehead makes you look like a sheriff's officer peerin' through a letterbox.'

A chap's strict diet had been successful, and he had lost many stones. But the transformation had not been achieved without facial evidence of a certain amount of strain. Or as a pal put it: 'I've seen healthier faces keekin' oot a coffin.'

A word about a senior Strathclyde policeman who shall remain nameless. He was introduced at a dinner with the information: 'He left school and joined the Navy – so the world could see him.'

We read that 'thousands of young women are losing their hair due to testosterone overload caused by taking on traditionally male roles in the workplace'. Further research by the Diary reveals other side effects to watch out for:
Marked improvement in driving skills.
Being on time.

TOM SHIELDS GOES FORTH 23

Spending significantly less than two hours a day in front of a mirror.

Happily wearing the same clothes on successive days.

Getting up and out in the morning in five minutes flat.

Being reasonable.

Having a phone conversation that lasts less time than a football match.

Finding it increasingly difficult to tear yourself away from the pub to catch the train home.

Joining in the snoring during *EastEnders*.

Developing a taste for the aphrodisiac qualities of eight pints of lager and a curry chaser.

Sam Galbraith, the Scottish Environment Minister and a few other things, while in a previous post as Scottish Health Minister was interviewed by the *Courier* newspaper which circulates in his Bearsden constituency. The questions to Sam, whose former day job was as a consultant neurosurgeon, included: 'Has working in the National Health Service made it any easier being the Minister for Health?' Sam answered: 'Yes, there's no doubt that having worked as a doctor helps. I know where the bodies are buried . . .'

The scene for this apparently true story is a holiday campsite in France. A five-a-side football tournament has been arranged, and many nationalities are involved.

A Scottish chap and his son find themselves pitted against a German. The German proves himself to be a skilful player. The Scotsman decides that the German requires to be 'closed down', as we believe is the technical term. A few hefty tackles have the desired effect of disconcerting the talented German. The Scottish chap urges his son to further discomfit the opponent with the words: 'Rummle him up! Rummle him up!' At which point the German walks off the park shouting: 'Will you British never forget the war?' Later investigation revealed that he thought the Scotsman was referring to Rommel.

THE FOLLOWING ITEM EXPOSES THE DIARY TO THE RISK OF THROWING STONES WHILE LIVING IN A GLASS HOUSE, BUT HERE GOES. IT CONSISTS OF EXTRACTS FROM A LIST OF JOURNALISTIC SOLECISM WHICH HAS BEEN COMPILED OVER THE YEARS.

There is one journalist, who shall remain nameless, who is the master of the neologism. He reported that a chap who would not take no for an answer was 'dogfastly' pursuing an issue. A new cinema multiplex was incorrectly but elegantly described as a 'multiflix'. The same man wrote of a 'florita of vessels on the river' and how a 'tirade of water flooded the playing fields'. He described a well-known local as 'a ken spectacle figure'. An accident victim, he said, had 'escaped the clutches of death's door', and a criminal who had ratted on his colleagues was quoted as saying: 'I could be dead the night before tomorrow.' 'Short-term jail sentences are getting longer,' he wrote. The unfortunate miners at Monktonhall 'faced a gauntlet of mixed emotions'.

Another expert at the mixed metaphor wrote: 'The Secretary of State must now pull the plug on the helpline before any more public money is literally poured down the telephone receiver.'

A feature writer explained: 'St Patrick, in case you didn't know, was the man responsible for driving all the snakes away from Ireland during the potato famine.' A travel article mentioned the joys of 'skiing in Cloisters'. A football writer reported that 'Tommy Burns venomously defended his goalkeeper.'

Scots often complain about English people moving to live north of the border. A correspondent put this in perspective: 'Interestingly, there is a situation where a disproportionate number of migratory Scots have alienated the indigenous community in the south-east of England by annexing top positions in business and the professions. They have become known as "piles": they are all right if they come down and go back up quickly. But if they come down and stay down, they are a pain in the posterior.'

There being so many *Big Issue* vendors around these days, each seller has to work hard at his or her marketing skills. Spotted outside Princes Square in Glasgow, a vendor whose pitch is: 'Get the Big Issue. Special competition. Star prize a week's timeshare in Easterhouse.' Another Glasgow vendor has taken to shouting: 'Big Issue. I take all major credit cards. Then I run away with them.'

Filched from the Internet; genuine (honest) announcements from US church bulletins:

Don't let worry kill you – let the church help.

On Thursday at 4 p.m., there will be an ice cream social. All ladies giving milk, please come early.

On Wednesday, the ladies' liturgy society will meet. Mrs Jones will sing 'Put me in my bed' accompanied by the pastor.

This being Easter Sunday, we will ask Mrs Lewis to come forward and lay an egg at the altar.

The service will close with 'Little drops of water'. One of the ladies will start (quietly) and the rest of the congregation will join in.

At the evening service tonight, the sermon topic will be 'What is hell?'. Come early and listen to our choir practise.

Weight Watchers will meet at 7 p.m. at the First Presbyterian Church. Please use the large double door at the side entrance.

The associate minister unveiled the church's new tithing campaign slogan last Sunday: 'I upped my pledge – up yours.'

SOMERFIELD
Clementines
Best eaten raw, peel off skin and break into segments

CLASS I

PACKED FOR SOMERFIELD STORES LTD,
PO BOX 708, BRISTOL BS99 1GA

More church magazine apocrypha: 'The ladies of the church have cast off clothing of all kinds. They can be seen in the church basement next Sunday.'

We hear of a Scottish minister who is not averse to taking a dram while on home visitations. In fact, his nickname is The Exorcist, because after his visit there are no spirits left in the house. And from the isle of Islay, we have a report of another minister who has got himself a new car. It is a French motor, a Citroën Temptation, which not a few of the locals consider a risqué little number for the minister.

For the dog who has everything, Petsmart, the shop for owners with more money than sense, is selling Santa suits and hats. The outfits come in all sizes to suit any breed. This will prevent the sort of dilemma suffered by a lady of the Diary's acquaintance, who decided to buy a new overcoat for her wee dug. She was trying to explain the size of her mutt when the woman in the pet shop suggested she bring the dog in so that the coat could be properly fitted. 'Oh, no, I couldn't do that,' the lady replied. 'It's a surprise for his birthday.'

The scene is a class in a primary school where a high heid yin has been dispatched to evaluate the level of English what the weans are being learnt. The inspector moves around the class having a discreet look at what the pupils are working on. He stops at a desk and asks the child for permission to read from her work:

'Today. Today. Today.

'Sad. Sad. Sad.

'Tomorrow. Tomorrow. Tomorrow.

'Hope. Hope. Hope.'

This is as fine a quatrain of poetry as he has seen, opines the high heid yin.

'Sir,' interrupts the child, 'that's my spelling practice.'

A Labour councillor at Glasgow City Chambers was reading (no word as to whether the lips were moving) an article in the *Herald* on proposed school closures. At the end of the article, in bold print, were the words 'Leader Comment – Page 21'.

The tribune of the people was seen to leaf through the newspaper and gaze intently at the page before saying: 'Frank McAveety is supposed to have an article on this page, but I can't find it.'

More wisdom of the school weans. A teacher has taken the class for a day in the country. The plan is to insinuate a bit of learning into the experience. Attempting to test one child's arithmetic, the teacher points to the field and asks: 'How many cows can you see?'

'All of them,' the pupil replies.

An overheard conversation, of the heated variety, between a couple who had fallen out seriously during a Christmas shopping expedition.

'Do you know what I would really like for Christmas?' she says.

'Tell me,' he snarls.

'A divorce.'

'I wasn't thinking of spending that much on you,' he replies.

A dispatch from the cut-throat, competitive world of Irish dancing. The Irish code, as all fans of *Riverdance* will know, requires that the hands are kept very still at the side of the body during the performance.

We hear of one young lad who was no mean dancer. His nimble and flashing feet made him a most promising candidate for the top prizes, at the highest levels of competition. The problem was that, in the heat of the action, he tended to lose control and his hands would deviate from the requisite stillness. His mother, whose ambition for her child knew no bounds, stitched the sleeves of his jacket to the sides so that the illegal movement could be curtailed.

All was going well until the lad fell over during a performance. He was, of course, unable to use his hands and arms to get up – a scenario which became obvious to the judges after a minute or so of the boy thrashing about on the floor as if he was in a straitjacket. Which, of course, he was. The lad, and his parents, were apparently subjected to the most condign punishment the Irish dancing hierarchy could impose, probably involving words such as *sine* and *die*.

A s meat regulations in Britain become ever stricter, it appears that anything goes in the good old US of A. A company called Scotsfare in Kansas City is trying to woo the American-Scottish exile community with a delicacy called the 'Haggis Pup'. Scotsfare say their Haggis Pups offer 'the flavor of Scotland for American tastes' and ask the obvious question: 'Why serve Polish sausage and brats at your Scottish events when you can offer traditional Scots sausage?'

Scotsfare make claims for their product which, if true, can only be described as an impressive feat of genetic engineering: 'A blend of lean pork and seasonings, Haggis Pups offer real haggis flavor but without the appetite-challenging ingredients of Burns's haggis.' Haggis Pups, we are told, are 'fully smoked and easily cooked' and, as a new Scottish food item, add authenticity to any Scottish gathering. All we can say is: 'Haggis? From a pig?'

T he scene is the boardroom of a Glasgow company where a number of wage slaves are gathered to be presented with gifts to mark 25 years' service. The boss makes a little speech about each employee, their interests and hobbies. There is a degree of puzzlement among the assembled staff as one of the recipients of the company's

-oOo-

A man was found lying on the ground motionless near the postbox in Russell Street last Monday.

An attempt to wake him by a local resident failed and the police were contacted.

On arrival, the man had woken up and was able to walk home unaccompanied.

munificence is asked if he plays in the orchestra and if he is still a football referee after all these years. The chap, well-known to his colleagues for his lack of any musical ability and famous for never at any time having been a football referee, had the good grace to blush.

We hear Ally McCoist has become rhyming slang among the ladies of this parish who are feeling, how can we put it, a bit frisky. They apparently refer to this sensation as 'I'm a bit Ally'. We didn't understand either until it was explained that both the letters C in his surname are silent in this connection.

An appropriate festive message spotted in the window of the Park Road Pharmacy, Kelvin-bridge, Glasgow: the words 'No well, no well.'

Award for worst Ne'er Day hangover goes to a chap in Cumbernauld, whose Hogmanay carousing was well up to his usual heroic standards. His dear wife found him next day with his head stuck in the wee foot spa-jacuzzi thing he had bought her for Christmas.

Runner-up is the punter who had a tumble in Edinburgh during the Hogmanay celebrations, and had to have attention in the casualty department. The treatment to his head-wound was administered with the new hi-tech stapling machine which has replaced stitches. Enquiries from concerned friends as to how the patient was doing were met with the answer: 'He's in a staple condition.'

A LADY CHEF, WHO WISHES TO REMAIN NAMELESS, FORWARDS THIS LIST OF TOP TEN REASONS WHY CHOCOLATE IS BETTER THAN SEX:

1. If you bite the nuts too hard the chocolate won't mind.
2. Chocolate satisfies even when it has gone soft.
3. You can safely have chocolate while you are driving.
4. You can make chocolate last as long as you want it to.
5. You can have chocolate even in front of your mother.
6. The word 'commitment' doesn't scare off chocolate.
7. When you have chocolate it doesn't keep the neighbours awake.
8. With chocolate, size doesn't matter; it's always good.
9. Good chocolate is easy to find.
10. You can have chocolate on your desk at work.

There were nine other reasons which we cannot repeat, but makes us wonder what lady chefs get up to these days.

Dermot MacQuarrie, a dear friend of the Diary and a very nearly kenspeckle Scottish television person, has settled in Los Angeles where he is an executive on a Spanish language sports channel. The big man, as we call him, has fitted in well to the Californian way of life, so much so that Dermot reports: 'Some people are saying I have gone very LA but my personal trainer, my publicist, and my herbalist disagree.'

Our award for services to the Burns Industry goes to a chap who organised a Rabbie supper in Iran. It was in the days when the Shah still ruled, so strong drink was allowed at the event. Under the influence of this strong drink, the organiser announced everyone had to 'sing a sang, tell a tale, show yer bum, or get oot'. He was eventually carried unconscious from the room, but not before seeing the Third Secretary (Commercial) of the British Embassy doff his breeks because he couldn't sing or tell jokes.

An accountant joke: How do you recognise an extrovert accountant? He's the one who stares at your shoes instead of his own when talking to you.

The scene is a German class at the school in Auchinleck. The teacher reminds her pupils to be sure to remember the umlauts on certain words. Her words have obviously struck home as, some minutes later, a pupil raises his hand to ask about a certain word. 'Is it wan o' thae words ah've got to put a wee omelette on the top?'

Every so often there is a debate about whether Scotland should have a new national anthem. The Diary nominates 'The Bluebell Polka' by Jimmy Shand. It is an extremely cheery wee number and just the job for getting the populace on their feet. Ideally, it will be played by a massed accordion and fiddle band with bagpipes expressly excluded. There is one problem. We will need new words to replace the existing verses which, as far as we know, go something like:

'Deedly dee dee deedle
'Deedle dee di doe.
'Deedly dee di deedle
'Deedle dee di doe.'

On second thoughts, these words will do just fine.

3. THE EVITAFICATION
OF DIANA

31 AUGUST 1998

This is a time for few words expressed eloquently. Prime Minister Tony Blair set the standard with his tribute to Diana as the 'People's Princess'. The sad reality is that Mr Blair's words will be a noble exception this week as the nation becomes mired in mawkish sentimentality. In the wake of the eloquent statesman, we had Richard and Judy on *This Morning*. 'Nice to see you in such awful circumstances,' Judy said, introducing the editor of *Majesty* magazine, wheeled on because she knew that Diana 'would want the world to know that she and Charles really loved each other'.

In the rush to inundate us with minute-by-minute coverage, the media are already providing a plethora of solecism. Diana's final resting place, the village church of Great Brington, Radio 5 tells us, will become 'a Mecca' for visitors. The ultimate irony is that Diana, a woman who lived by the media and, they are claiming, died by the media, will receive the most comprehensive media send-off in

饮　用　水
DRINKING　WATER
热⬅　➡冷
HOT　　　COLD
经检疫部门检验合格
PASSED BY QUARANTINE AUTHORITES

history. Diana was the biggest star in the top soap opera in the world and as students of soap opera know, the biggest ratings boosts always coincide with sudden and tragic deaths.

The bad news for those of even a remotely republican persuasion is that the normal life of the nation must stop until this sad Princess is laid to rest. I am too young and unversed in royal funeral protocol to recall what happened when the old King died; presumably there was dignified music on the TV and radio and public events were cancelled. But what kind of mourning is it when football matches are cancelled but Richard and Judy carry on broadcasting, conducting inane interviews with pundits who make a living from the royal industry – pundits who are probably profiting even more than florists from the extravagant expressions of public grief which have accompanied the death of this young woman. A performance of *Only An Excuse*, a football comedy show, is cancelled at the King's Theatre in Glasgow. The Scottish Football Association dithers over whether to go ahead with the World Cup qualifying match against Belarus. Meanwhile, the Braemar Gathering has been cancelled.

The world has changed since the last King died. In the early 1950s it may have been possible to have a respectful week of mourning before the state funeral of a royal personage, but the royal circus has moved on a considerable distance since then. The media are in the process of beatifying, canonising, and deifying Diana in short order. Surely not long delayed will be her Evitafication. Work will have already started on the script for the film, the video, and the musical. The truth is that Diana the musical would be a more appropriate remembrance than Diana the state funeral. She is more Elton John than Elgar. More glitz and glamour than pomp and panoply. Some TV channels have spotted this and have taken to filling the gaps between news bulletins with images of this beautiful young woman to the background noise of trite pop songs. 'I Will Always Love You' is probably the most nauseous, so far.

Diana had become a commodity, a valuable currency in the entertainment industry. On Radio 4's *News Quiz* programme on Saturday afternoon, she was the butt of a succession of withering jokes. The next day she was dead and revered, and the national anthem was being played on the hour. BBC radio said in its news bulletin that Diana was a tragic figure who had suffered from over-exposure in the media. They then announced that Radios 1, 2, 3, 4,

 **TOM SHIELDS GOES FORTH** 35

and 5 Live would immediately merge to give continuous coverage of the story.

BBC television, charged with the duty of providing sober and stately coverage, portrayed Diana not as a royal soap star turned saint, but as Diana the icon. This slightly more upmarket use of Greek words set them just a notch or two above Richard and Judy. In their search to fill the hours of broadcasting, the BBC took recourse to showbiz. Billy Connolly and his wife, Pamela Stephenson, were called upon to comment. Billy is best known these days for his role as John Brown in the film about Queen Victoria, *Mrs Brown*, which shows that showbiz can stalk royalty well beyond the grave. To be fair to Billy, he kept his comments brief, touching and honest. He had met Diana and liked her – he hadn't realised just how much until she was gone.

It will be an arduous week as the media hype increases. British TV, radio, and print may attempt to be dignified, but we will not wager too heavily on this. The foreign media will have no such qualms. Most importantly, from a Scottish point of view, is the possibility of our devolution referendum being placed in jeopardy. The last two weeks of campaigning will have effectively been lost. There is a grave danger of a royalist-sentimentalist swing against a Yes vote by some who may think that in the wake of the death of the Princess Britain needs unity, equalling union.

The demise of Princess Diana is immensely sad. She was a caring person, a defender of the underdog, and undoubtedly a People's Princess. Who knows what she might have achieved if she had stuck to the task of being the very perfect model of a modern British queen? The reality is that she was the perfect example of what can happen when you marry into the wrong family. Most of all, Diana's demise is the ultimate warning about getting into a car which is being driven far too fast by a man who has had too much to drink.

4. WALK THIS WAY

HOW TO LIVE WITH ORANGE PARADES: A DIARY GUIDE FOR THOSE WHO ARE ALLERGIC TO THE WALK

Be tolerant; it may be catching. Ask yourself what is wrong with a good walk on a summer's day, with a bit of incidental music. Greet the walkers with a cheery wave and a word of welcome. If it is raining, however, do not say: 'It's a nice day for it.'

Try to understand the Orange Order's point of view. Realise that more is likely to be achieved by engaging in a dialogue. Realise also that it might take generations before any mutual understanding is reached. While taking this long-term view, do not at any time observe to an Orangeman that 'Rome wasn't built in a day.'

Try to learn the words of some of the Orange tunes. They are quite catchy, although it can take years to perfect the shoulder movements. Do not ask the band if they know the 'Fields of Athenry'.

Accept the Orange Order's inalienable right to march anywhere and hold up traffic. Do not say that if it was up to you, it would be compulsory for them to march every day of the year for at least 18 hours at a time.

Buy a Union Flag and join the crowds watching from the pavement. Use the opportunity to buy a large carry-out of cheap wine, strong lager, and alcopops. It's not every day you can blatantly break the laws banning drinking in public and know that the police will do nothing to stop you.

Treat the Walk as an opportunity to overcome any inhibitions about urinating in public places. Go on, admit it, you've always wanted to pish copiously against a bus shelter in the High Street in broad daylight.

Look upon the Walk as one giant street party. Set out tables with glasses of orange juice for the marchers to slake their thirst as they pass. Some street entertainment, such as clowns and jugglers, would be appropriate.

Engage the Orange celebrators in a discussion about their great hero, King Billy. Try to avoid, however, pointing out to the Sons of William flute band that William was homosexual and had no offspring.

Best also skirt around that bit of history where King Billy and the Pope were allies and how the Vatican were well pleased with the result of the Battle of the Boyne.

Take a positive attitude to the Orange Walk as a colourful spectacle. Tell the women how nice they look and marvel at the number of bright shades of crimplene available these days.

Dept of Talking Balls. Hearts manager Jim Jefferies, explaining to listeners to Radio Scotland why his goalkeeper Gilles Rousset wasn't playing one weekend: 'He's still feeling his groin.'

Overheard in an Edinburgh cinema, where the audience are engrossed in watching *Titanic*: the big boat has hit the iceberg and is shipping water at a great rate. Member of audience to friend: 'The ship's gonny sink.' Friend: 'Naw it wullnae.'

The scene is the Clydesdale Bank in Corstorphine, Edinburgh, where a dear old lady is making a production number of her visit to the bank, as dear old ladies do. The lady's conversation with the young girl behind the counter covers all sorts of topics, from decorating to shopping. Having enjoyed her chat, the lady is set to leave but not before a final pleasantry. 'That's a lovely name. Is it French?' The girl looks at her badge and explains that Trainee is her job description, not her name.

BOVINE DEFINITIONS OF FORMS OF GOVERNMENT.

Feudalism: You have two cows. Your feudal superior takes some of the milk.

Pure socialism: You have two cows. The government takes them and puts them in a barn with everyone else's cows. You have to take care of all the cows. The government gives you as much milk as you need.

Bureaucratic socialism: You have two cows. The government takes them and puts them in a barn with everyone else's cows. They are cared for by ex-chicken farmers. You have to take care of the chickens the government took from the chicken farmers. The government gives you as much milk and as many eggs as the regulations say you should need.

Fascism: You have two cows. The government takes both, hires you to take care of them, and sells you the milk.

American democracy: The government promises to give you two cows if you vote for it. After the election, the president is impeached for speculating in cow futures. The press dubs the affair Cowgate.

British democracy: You have two cows. You feed them sheeps' brains and they go mad. The government doesn't do anything.

Totalitarianism: You have two cows. The government takes them and denies they ever existed. Milk is banned.

Capitalism: You have two cows. You sell one and buy a bull.

Hong Kong capitalism: You have two cows. You sell three of them to a publicly listed company, using letters of credit opened by your brother-in-law at the bank, then execute a debt/equity swap with associated general offer so that you get all four cows back, with a

 **TOM SHIELDS GOES FORTH**

tax deduction for keeping five cows. The milk rights of six cows are transferred via a Panamanian intermediary to a Cayman Islands company secretly owned by the majority shareholder, who sells the rights to all seven cows' milk back to the listed company. The annual report says that the company owns eight cows, with an option on one more. Meanwhile, you kill the two cows because the feng shui is bad.

Feminism: You have two cows. They get married and adopt a veal calf.

Environmentalism: You have two cows. The government bans you from milking or killing them.

At a prestigious dinner in Edinburgh a senior establishment figure, surveying the many top people present, felt constrained to say that there had not been such a concentration of intelligentsia, academia, and colossi of the corridors of power present 'since the last time Derry Irvine dined alone'.

The scene is a garden in the douce West End of Glasgow where a spot of afternoon tea is being taken outdoors, the weather being so awfy clammy. The man of the house is stung by a wasp but is taking it all quite calmly. He calls through the open windae to his dear wife to pass him some vinegar to treat the sting.

'Do you want ordinary or balsamic?' his West End lady replies.

Sign in a cafe in Largs: 'Canned drinks now available to sit in.'

The joys of sponsorship. Q96, Paisley's rockingest radio station, had a phone-in competition on a sporting theme. The prize, put up by Adidas, was a pair of their football boots or a £50 voucher for a sports shop. The winner opted for the £50 voucher. 'And what will you spend it on?' asked the presenter.

'I'll put it towards a better pair of football boots,' was the reply.

You can take the girl out of Glasgow but you can't take Glasgow out of the girl. On a visit to the city by the Orient Express, Glesga keelies with £150 a head to spare could sample the delights of the famous train on a quick evening jaunt around Central Scotland. The £150 a skull

included much free drink, and great efforts were made to obtain value for money, so much so that in one case first aid was required.

An eye witness reported that at least one lady passenger felt she needed further value for money. She purloined eight bars of Orient Express soap, which she secreted in her bra. Another nice souvenir was the complete set of Orient Express cutlery. We have no information as to where this was hidden.

The *In Touch* magazine of Lenzie Rugby Club had a question-and-answer piece with one of their players, Martin Stewart. Asked to describe his most embarrassing moment, he replied it was when fellow player George Barber asked Mrs Martin 'How's the crack?' two weeks after she had given birth. It should be pointed out that Mr Barber is Irish.

Some citizens are less than committed to their local football team – like the lady in one of the houses adjacent to the Rugby Park training ground in Kilmarnock. During the team's training one night, the stadium manager was summoned urgently by the goalkeeper. The ball had gone over the garden fence and

requests from the keeper were met by the lady of the house replying: 'I've told you before, you're not getting your ball back.'

A return to the murky water of the malapropism. A reader reports a colleague at a staff meeting who urged that everyone should be 'singing from the same spreadsheet'. He also admitted that on one issue he was 'a bit of a doubting Joseph'.

The transgressions of Scottish schoolchildren thankfully continue to be mostly of a minor nature. A Port Glasgow teacher reports that, as she was supervising the line of pupils first thing one morning, a ten-year-old boy pushed half a dozen bedraggled daffodils into her hands with the words: 'Here, miss, these are fur you. Ah would huv goat mair but the wumman banged oan the windae.'

An insight into the characteristics of various nations is offered by the following scenario. Imagine a series of desert islands in the middle of nowhere. On each island are stranded two Italian men and one Italian woman, two French men and one French woman, and similar complements of Germans, Greeks, English, Bulgarian, Swedish and Irish.

One month later on these respective little havens of paradise, one of the Italian men has killed his compatriot to have the Italian woman for himself.

The two French men and the French woman are living happily together in a *menage à trois*.

The Germans have set up a strict weekly rota.

The two Greek men are sleeping with each other and the Greek woman is cleaning and cooking for them.

The English men are waiting for someone to introduce them to the English woman, while the English woman has swum over to a neighbouring island and is hanging out with the natives.

The Bulgarian men took one look at the endless ocean, one look at the Bulgarian woman and started swimming.

The two Swedish men are contemplating the virtues of suicide while the woman reiterates that her body is her own. But at least it's not snowing and the taxes are low.

The Irish, meanwhile, have divided the island into North and South and have set up a distillery. They haven't got round to talking to the Irish woman yet.

The scene is the Glasgow-Aberdeen train, where a traveller is feeling peckish and is tempted by a banana muffin. But, wary of the high prices of items on rail buffet trolleys, he asks of the girl: 'Are these muffins exorbitant?'

'I don't know,' she replies. 'I've never tasted them.'

Glaswegian overheard dispensing pearl of wisdom to friend: 'Och, it's aw much ae a muchness, hen. Six o' wan and and two-thirds o' the other . . .'

What do you get when you cross an alsatian with a mason? A police dog with excellent prospects of promotion.

What do you get if you cross a skinhead with a Jehovah's Witness? Someone who knocks on your door and tells you to feck off.

An archaeological tale. German scientists dug 50ft underground and discovered small pieces of copper. They announced that the ancient Germans, 25,000 years ago, had a nationwide telephone network. British scientists dug even deeper and 100ft down they found small pieces of glass. They announced that 35,000 years ago, ancient

Britons had a nationwide fibre-optic telephone network. The Irish dug 200ft underground. They found absolutely nothing and announced that the ancient Irish, 55,000 years ago, were using cellular telephones.

Spotted in the sightseeing heart of Rome: a cafe with a definite Scottish influence. The window bears two hand-written signs; the first, 'Tea is served here' and the other, much more prominent, 'Skip the Trevi, have a bevvy.'

True answers from the important TV quiz show *Family Fortunes*.
'Name a bird with a long neck.' 'Naomi Campbell.'
'Something in the garden that's green.' 'My shed.'
On to sport –
'Name a dangerous race.' 'The Arabs.'

JAPANESE BANKING.

It would appear that the Origami Bank has folded, and the Sumo Bank has gone belly-up. The Bonsai Bank's growth has been stunted and now it will have to have some of its branches cut back. Meanwhile, the Karaoke Bank is up for sale and is (wait for it) going for a song, while shares in the Kamikaze Bank have nosedived and the directors of the Bank of Nippon have nipped off.

Five hundred at the Karate Bank got the chop, and there is something distinctly fishy going on at the Sushi Bank. Staff there fear a raw deal. The only rising sun ray of light in all this is news of a new bank rising from the ashes, Hiroshima Savings, with its slogan: 'We've survived worse.'

Geisha break, please.

MORE JAPANESE BANKING.

The Sayonara Bank is now apparently a good buy. And staff at the Kimono Bank have been called in for a dressing down.

It would be tasteless to poke fun at the plight of the Tofu Bank. Not much is being said about the demise of the Haiku Bank, apparently only 17 words at a time. Despite their hands-on approach, the Shiatsu Bank just can't put their finger on what's going wrong. In the Fuji Bank, all the meetings are being held in camera.

Also in the Far East, the governors of the Shih-Tzu Bank are barking mad because the place has gone to the dogs. At the Kowtow Bank they will bend over forwards to please the customers. Over at the Samurai and Hari-Kiri Banks, the staff are still too cut up to talk. At the Tamagochi Bank the customers have died through lack of interest.

Finally, at the Jujitsu Bank they just don't give a toss any more.

We hear of a Newton Mearns lady who, intent upon changing the predictable course of her relationship with her husband, suggested one evening they try a new position. The husband was eminently agreeable to this.

'OK,' she said, 'you get up here and do the ironing and I'll lie down on the sofa and watch television.'

THIS PARODY OF BOHEMIAN RHAPSODY WAS FILCHED FROM THE INTERNET, BUT IT IS OFTEN REQUESTED AS A REPEAT BY DIARY READERS. IT IS QUEEN WITH A DISTINCT CURRY FLAVOUR. SING ALONG:

> 'Naan, I just killed a man,
> Poppadom against his head,
> Had lime pickle, now he's dead.'

We move on to such lyrics as 'Curry on, curry on, because nothing really Madras' and 'Goodbye, every bhaji, I've got to go, gotta leave you all behind and use the loo.'

And we find ourselves after the guitar solo at the really fast bit:

> 'I see a little chicken tikka on the side,
> Rogan Josh, Rogan Josh, pass the chutney made of mango.
> Vindaloo does nicely, very very spicey indeed!
> Biryani (Biryani), Biryani (Biryani) Biryani and a naan.
> (A vindaloo loo loo . . .) loo loo loo loo loo loo loo.
> I've eaten balti, somebody help me,
> (He's eaten balti, get him to a lavatory)
> Stand you well back, 'cos this loo is quarantined.'

We hesitate to print more but we can say that the song ends with the phrase 'any way the wind blows'.

DEEP THOUGHTS.

If man evolved from apes, why do we still have apes?

The main reason Santa is so jolly is because he knows where all the bad girls live.

If a mute swears, does his mother wash his hands with soap?

Whose cruel idea was it for the word lisp to have the letter 's' in it?

If a man is in the middle of the forest speaking and there is no woman around to hear him, is he still wrong?

If a man does the ironing in the middle of a forest and there is no woman standing behind him watching, will he still be doing it wrong?'

Isn't it a bit unnerving that doctors call what they do 'practice'?

What do you do when you see an endangered animal eating an endangered plant?

If the police arrest a mime artist, do they tell him he has the right to remain silent?

We hear from Los Angeles of Helen Mclean, a Glasgow woman who has made a new life out there but in 25 years has still not lost her accent. She has a career as a realtor. Yes, she sells houses quite successfully despite, during her sales spiel, uttering such statements as: 'And jist look at thae big windaes.'

Helen's children have picked up some of the accent from her, and are apt to come in from a hard day's play with such comments as: 'Gee, mom, ah'm a' clatty.' The weans are staunch supporters of their mum's Glasgow connections. They love Irn Bru and black pudding. But their Scottish heritage was put to a pretty stern test when they first went to school and a cultural difference set them apart.

They were the only kids in the class whose schoolbooks were covered in wallpaper.

An apocryphal and largely unlikely tale, but we will pass it on anyway.

It concerns a chap who is required to take along a sperm sample to a fertility clinic in Glasgow. He is advised by telephone that he should 'put the test tube in a warm pocket'. The patient decides to take no chances. He arrives and hands the receptionist a foil-wrapped package. When opened, the contents emit a quantity of steam. The staff had never before seen a test-tube sample nestling in a baked potato.

GRAMPIAN REGIONAL COUNCIL

TOUGH SCHOOL

A cowboy is sitting in a Sauchiehall Street pub – spurs, stetson, pistol, jeans, the lot. A young lady asks him: 'Are you a real cowboy?'

'Yer durn tootin'. Spent ma whole life ridin' the range, herdin' critters, breakin' horses, shootin' outlaws. Say, what are you, ma'am?'

'Me?' she says. 'I'm a lesbian.'

'Ah ain't never heerd o' that,' he says. 'What's a lesbian?'

She explains: 'Well, I'm attracted to women and think about them all the time.' The lesbian goes into some detail, which need not concern us here, of her obsession with beautiful women.

The young lady leaves. The cowboy is sat there ponderin' when an elderly lady approaches him and asks: 'Are you a real cowboy?'

'Well, ma'am, I always thought I was but I guess I've just found out I'm a lesbian.'

The politically incorrect zone. Why doesn't Mexico have an Olympic team? Because everybody who can run, jump and swim is already in the US.

How do you make five pounds of fat look good? Put a nipple on it.

If your wife keeps coming out of the kitchen to nag you, what have you done wrong? Made her chain too long.

The scene is a school in Lanarkshire where a teacher has finally lost patience with an otherwise able pupil who insists on using the phrase 'I have wrote'. She keeps him behind to copy 'I have written' 100 times.

She is called to see the headmaster, and upon her return finds that the lad has finished his punishment exercise.

He has left his piece of paper with an accompanying note which says: 'Miss, I have wrote I have written 100 times and I have went home.'

A chap is driving along in his car when his boss rings up to tell him he has been promoted. He is surprised by the move, loses concentration, and swerves.

Further along the road, the boss rings to say he has been promoted again. The driver manages to control an even more serious swerve.

The boss rings up a third time and says: 'You have been appointed

managing director.' At which point our man swerves and hits a tree.

'What happened to you?' asks the policeman attending the scene. 'I careered off the road,' was the reply.

A slightly blasphemous tale. The scene is a council house in Nazareth, where Joseph has a thundering hangover having returned from a marriage feast at Cana. Mary offers black coffee and/or an Abdine powder, which Joseph declines with a request to just let him die in peace. 'You're dehydrated,' Mary says. 'How about a long drink of cool water straight from the well?'

'A good idea,' says Joseph. 'But don't send the boy for it.'

A golfer visits the doctor for treatment to a slight arthritic pain in his wrist. He is prescribed a medicine called Voltarol, which we are sure is the finest treatment your prescription money can buy. Our man was slightly concerned by the warning note on side effects which accompanied the Voltarol: 'Occasionally, Voltarol can cause stomach pain, nausea, vomiting, diarrhoea, indigestion, wind, loss of appetite, headaches, dizziness and skin rashes.

'On rare occasions, it can cause gastric ulcers, peptic ulcers, gastro-intestinal bleeding (bleeding when emptying your bowels), tiredness and drowsiness, kidney or liver problems, jaundice (yellowing of the skin), oedema (fluid retention), hypotension (lightheadedness or fainting) and wheezing.

'On very rare occasions, it can cause constipation, glossitis (sore tongue), mouth ulcers, sore throat, numbness in the fingers, tremors. Skin rashes which may be made worse by sunlight or sunlamps have been reported, as well as blurred vision, hearing loss, tinnitus (ringing in the ears), disorientation, loss of memory, insomnia, irritability, anxiety, depression, mood changes, nightmares, convulsions, alteration of taste, loss of hair, hypertension (high blood pressure), palpitations, chest pain and headaches accompanied by a dislike of bright lights and a stiff neck.

'Blood changes may also occur. If you notice that you are bruising more easily, have frequent infections or sore throats, tell your doctor.

'Do not be alarmed by this list – most people take Voltarol without any problems.'

Or you could give up golf.

We fear that there is still some work to be done political correctness-wise in the douce Glasgow inner suburb of Possil. A reader who had occasion to enter a chip shop in this barrio spotted an item on the menu listed as a 'Paki Bridie'. Asked to give more detail of this delicacy, the chip shop owner held up a samosa.

Myra Paton of Bishopbriggs started something when she sent us the label which adorned her purchase of mince from Safeway. The mince was described as 'ideal for recipes'. Myra wrote: 'Perhaps you can solve the riddle of this label. What else can you use mince for apart from recipes? Perhaps stuffing it into certain football shirts now that the season is upon us?'

We put the Diary Brains Trust onto this question and they came up with a few suggestions for alternative uses for mince:

Form it into paragraphs and make a *Herald* Diary.
Mould it into hand grenades and perpetrate lightning attacks on vegetarian restaurants.
In the absence of snow, use mince for summer snowball fights.

Choose mince as the medium for a new statue in George Square,
    possibly in honour of a civic leader.
Construct your own Edinburgh Festival.
Construct your own Scottish Parliament.
If you are really stuck for ideas, you could cook the mince and serve
    it with mashed potatoes and marrowfat peas. Or, as a reader
    suggested, the mince could be 'pan-fried in its own *jus* and served
    with pot-boiled potatoes'.

A vignette in a Glasgow street, where an elderly couple have
obviously been having a disagreement. She is walking a few yards
in front of him. She turns round abruptly and says: 'Just you stop
right there!' Her man duly does so. She wags a finger in his face and
asks: 'When did I ever shift your teeth?' A glance at the man reveals
the gummy visage of one who is *sans* dentures, the whereabouts of
the aforementioned tap set obviously being the reason for the
marital warfare.

5. MEJOR TARDE QUE NUNCA

5 NOVEMBER 1998

You know you have taken a wee bit too long over your university career when you turn up for the graduation ceremony and the principal is looking very young. Please forgive a touch of self-indulgence but I feel that, having taken 32 years to get a degree from Strathclyde University, I should have the chance to mention it in passing.

To emphasise the *Guinness Book of Records*-length of pursuit of my degree, fate would have it that at the graduation ceremony this week I should meet Bill Copland who started with me at Strathclyde in October 1966. Bill was there for a family graduation. While I was taking all this time over a degree – and a wee degree at that, none of your Hons – Bill had graduated, followed a glittering career in the world of further education, and has now retired.

Let me tell you, there is nothing quite as haunting as an unfinished degree course. For years after I left Strathclyde University in 1969, two credits short of my maths and engineering degree, I

suffered nightmares. These involved examinations in lecture theatres I couldn't find. If you found the exam room, the questions appeared to be in Greek or Russian. The nightmares came from my being the first person in my family ever to go to university. My father, an old Labour man, passionately espoused education, education, education, long before Tony Blair made it a glib phrase and an undelivered election pledge. It was hell to let him down. He never said a word of criticism. The closest he got to chiding was when I tried and failed to open a tin of corned beef for the tea. These tins with the keys can be very complicated, after all. 'Engineering, was it, you studied?' he asked. Engineering and mathematics was, on reflection, not the best career path.

I turned my back on the white heat of technology and opted for the glamour and big bucks of working for the *Sunday Post*. But the fates were kind. In 1992 I met John Arbuthnot, the youthful principal of Strathclyde Yoonie. He exhorted me to return to finish my degree. Even better, I was able to shun mathematics and technical stuff and top up my degree by studying Spanish, Catalan, and Beverage Management. (The last subject is basically wine-tasting and can be enjoyed as part of a rounded education at Strathclyde University's Hotel School.)

Having completed my second spell at Strathclyde, I can say that everyone should go to university twice. Once in the first flush of youth and again in your 40s or 50s, when you can really enjoy it. If I had stuck in at the maths and engineering, I wouldn't have had the pleasure of being bought my graduation lunch by my children. There's nothing quite as gratifying as getting a return on the graduation lunches you had to buy your weans.

If I had graduated back in 1970, the lunch would most likely have been in a steakhouse with a bottle of cheap plonk, but with the benefit of my life experience as a lunching journalist and that patina of sophistication from the beverage management course, I was able to opt for the gambas and the sea bass at Tony Matteo's City Merchant bistro. And a bottle or 12 of Mount Riley, an excellent New Zealand sauvignon blanc to which I have been introduced by Alan Chapman of Waverley Vintners.

I will miss being a student: not least the 10 per cent discount off my fruit and veg at Roots and Fruits and the concession prices to get into the cinema. And, if I hadn't been back at the studying, I would

have had no excuse whatsoever to wander into the Strathclyde students' union on cheeze night. That's how us students spell cheese nowadays. Cheeze is the Thursday night club at the Union, where there are special offers on After Shock and designer beers, and very loud music. As you read this I will most likely be feeling cheezed out, having celebrated my farewell to Strathclyde University. Until the next time.

6. THE NIGHT YOU STOLE MY TEETH

Dr John Reid, MP for Dark Bits of North Lanarkshire, and ex-Secretary of State for Scotland makes sure he maintains outside interests, such as following Celtic. During a Labour Party conference he was faced with the serious dilemma of being in Brighton while his team were playing Liverpool at Anfield in the UEFA Cup.

In an inspired moment, the then Armed Forces Minister got Mary, his redoubtable constituency secretary, to pencil in a very important engagement in his diary for that evening. She wrote truthfully: '7pm: defence, future goals and Europe'.

More on dentures as a source of conflict between Scottish married folk. The scene is a bar in Motherwell where a couple are sitting in frosty silence, suddenly broken by the man saying: 'Aye, but whit aboot that night you stole ma teeth so ah couldnae sing in the karaoke.'

A cannibal and his young son are walking along the beach when they encounter a lovely young woman, recently shipwrecked.

'Dad, Dad!' says the wee boy. 'Can we take her home and eat her? Can we, Dad?'

'I don't think so, son,' says Dad. 'But I've got a better idea. Let's take her home and eat your mammy.'

Overheard: 'I'm no' saying she's fat but when she threw her knickers on to the stage at a Sydney Devine concert, Sydney thought the safety curtain had come doon.'

A sign, handwritten, on the door of the Bay Cafe in Rothesay: 'Toilets are solely for the use of sit-in patrons.' Another sign, a proper metal one and very artistic, in Dunoon. It says: 'Welcome to Dunoon – home of Dunoon mugs.'

It appears that Glasgow's mental young boys are becoming adept at marketing. Spotted in the underpass at Finnieston below the Clydeside Expressway, this slogan sprayed in 6-inch black letters: 'Bored? Nothing worth watching on television? Then why not join your local street gang. Ibrox Young Team.'

The scene is a Glasgow court, where the accused is vehemently denying a charge of shoplifting. The problem, as is so often the case, is that the prosecution have a videotape which shows quite clearly the accused in the act of purloining the goods in question.

The accused watches the video which, incontrovertibly, has footage of himself stuffing the items up his jook.

He appears despondent.

Suddenly he cheers up considerably, and even leaps to his feet in elation.

'Look,' he cries. 'I put the stuff back.'

'Naw, son, we're jist rewind-

ing the tape,' says the court officer.

An employment opportunity advertised on the notice board at a Glasgow Safeway store. The post is described as 'ambient replenishment'. Or shelf-stacking, as it used to be known.

We hear of a Kleeneze catalogue which advertises a rubber bathmat as 'ideal for use in the bath'.

English, as she is translated from foreign tongues.

In the Lutfen Hotel, Havlurarini, Turkey, a notice advises: 'While on fire, meet everybody in the road.'

The location for this tale is Arduthie Primary School in Stonehaven, where the kids are fairly well brung up. A wee girl says: 'Miss, Ian just said the C word.' Ian gets hauled out and, looking pretty guilty, gets a full dressing down in front of the class. When it's all finished, the teacher says: 'Well, what have you got to say for yourself?'

Ian, almost in tears by this time, says: 'Miss, I only said "Christmas".'

SAREHOLE SURGERY

Another tale of Ayrshire education. The scene is the Gael Motor Group East Ayrshire Secondary Schools Quiz, organised by the Kilmarnock Round Table (no sponsor goes unmentioned in this Diary). It was won by Loudoun Academy of Galston. The highlight was provided by a fourth-year representative of Grange Academy, Kilmarnock. He was asked: 'What can be Black, Red, or Dead?' The expected answer was 'Seas'. The young man replied: 'A penguin in a liquidiser.'

A tale, most likely apocryphal, from the island of Tiree. The phone rings in the local post office. It is a London journalist from the *Times* newspaper, trying to find someone who can tell him the results of a wind-surfing championship which was being held on the island. 'Hello,' says the journalist, 'I'm from the *Times*.' The Tiree person interjects: 'Would that be the *Oban Times* or the *Piping Times*?'

A Drumcree tale. A flying saucer lands in the Garvachy Road. A small orange-coloured extra-terrestrial gets out and is confronted by a local resident, who asks: 'What the hell are you?'

'I'm a Martian,' says the ET.

'Not down this road you're not,' replies the resident.

The scene is an ante-natal class full of pregnant women and their partners. The instructor is teaching the women how to breath properly, along with informing the men how to give the necessary assurances at this stage of the plan. The teacher then announces: 'Ladies, exercise is good for you. Walking is especially beneficial. And, gentlemen, it wouldn't hurt you to take the time to go walking with your partner!'

A man raises his hand and asks: 'Is it all right if she carries a golf bag while we walk?'

A librarian at Glasgow's Mitchell Library was having trouble with a ballpoint pen which only worked properly if you leaned heavily on it. When he passed it to a member of the public making a request for a book, he could see she was having difficulty with it, so he told her: 'Put your weight on it.' The puzzled woman paused, and then wrote '12st 3lbs' on the request form.

A certain product has been the subject of some discussion in Frasers cosmetics depart-

ment. The problematic unguent is by Aveda, an American company, and is designed to give protection from the ravages of household chores. 'I do so wish they hadn't called it "Hand Relief",' one of the Frasers sales ladies is reported as saying.

A Glasgow girl, just a common wee Glasgow girl, starts a new job as a waitress at a restaurant where the clients can be a poco pretencioso. The customer asks for his vegetables to be served *al dente*. She tells the chef she thinks he wants his veg done the way his 'auld auntie' does it.

N ews on the British Telecom friends and family front. A married lady of this parish was conducting an affair. To avoid her paramour's telephone number appearing on the on the itemised conjugal bill, she would make a brief call and her lover would phone back. The ever-vigilant BT computer noted that while each call cost very little, the frequency merited an entry at number three in the friends and family top ten. The ensuing marital mayhem at least brought some business for private investigators and divorce lawyers.

SOME CHARACTERISTICS WHICH MIGHT HELP TO DEFINE YOUR GLASWEGIAN ORIGINS:

You've never had your tea in Edinburgh.
Your forehead gets bruised when you kiss somebody.
You've never shoved yer granny aff a bus.
You know that Barraland is not an African state.
You know that Huns aren't necessarily Germanic.
You know that jeely is not an Italian opera singer.
You know that Buckie might not mean a northern town.
You know that jellies are not always plates full of wobbly stuff to be given to kids.
You know that herries are not German gentlemen.
You know that the Bar-L is not something to be rolled out.

 **TOM SHIELDS GOES FORTH**

The scene is a Little Chef in deepest Ayrshire, where a customer has ordered the soup of the day. 'What is the soup?' he asks as an afterthought. The waitress replies that she doesn't know. When she returns with a bowl of soup, she confesses that she still cannot identify which variety it is. The soup does not immediately identify itself from appearance, aroma or flavour. Now thoroughly intrigued, the customer asks to talk to the chef.

'What is the soup?' he asks the chef who has appeared in full cook's regalia. 'I don't know,' he replies. 'It comes in a plain brown packet.'

Jim Murphy, New Labour MP for Eastwood, tells of his unsuccessful efforts to make his maiden speech in the Commons. His proud mum and dad were over from South Africa for the occasion. They took their lad out for a decent lunch to fortify him for the occasion of his first address to the country.

Oor Jim waited and waited to speak as dozens of new MPs hovered on the edges of their seats like aircraft stacked over Heathrow. Some hours into the waiting period, Mr Murphy began to feel the pressure of all the drink he had consumed at lunch. Soft drinks, we have to say. Mr Murphy treats his body as a temple. He was pure burstin', as they say in Eastwood, and a wee bit beelin' as well, as a Tory maiden speaker went on interminably about how he was the umpteenth generation of his family to represent his seat.

Just as Jim rose to head for the lavatory, did not Betty Boothroyd fix him with a look and summon him to make his speech? Mr Murphy said nothing. 'Mr Murphy, are you willing?' she asked. 'Willing but unable, Madam Speaker,' he replied and exited in search of relief.

The Hansard shorthand writers can be kind to MPs who find themselves in dilemmas, and edit out some detail. The Hansard report for Mr Murphy's aborted speech merely states: 'Mr Murphy rose...'

FUTHER CHARACTERISTICS WHICH MIGHT HELP TO DEFINE YOUR GLASWEGIAN ORIGINS:

You don't get excited by a 44D.
The subway makes you dizzy.
You think of ginger without Fred.
You think *Paradise Lost* is Mo Johnston's autobiography.
You think teddy bears are blue.

Sheikh Hasina, Prime Minister of Bangladesh, was due in Dundee to celebrate the jute tradition, enlisted to officially open the second phase of the city's Verdant jute museum. Organisers of the state visit were surprised when a Bangladeshi security official turned up and asked, among other questions, what arrangements had been made for a food-taster to be on hand. One seasoned observer of Dundee civic beanfeasts remarked: 'They needn't worry. There's bound to be a few councillors into the buffet before her.'

A Glaswegian called Pat Rice moves to Dundee. He marries, produces progeny and duly receives advice from a local on what not to call his newborn son. 'Don't call him Fred,' he is told. 'Fred Rice is something Dundonians order in a Chinese restaurant.'

Any venture by the Diary into the lingua franca of Dundee produces a flurret (that's a small flurry) of contributions. Lesley Fuller recalled her student days, which involved the culture shock of moving from Kilmacolm to Clootie City. She was often fazed by the accent, particularly the word 'fred' in its culinary context. 'One evening some friends and I came upon a chippie in the "Hulltoon" area. One entire wall of this establishment was decorated with pictures of Fred Flintstone, and a large caption in the middle of the wall informed the customer that "A'thing in this shop is Fred!"

'It took me quite a few minutes to work that one out. I also learned that a Danish pastry is called a "Fred Egg" – eminently more appropriate if it is of the yellow custard variety.'

Alan Arnott wrote: 'I remember a pub lunch in Dundee with a waitress shouting orders through the hatch to the kitchen. An order which pleased us greatly was, "A peh, a peh, a peh, a bridie, an' a peh".'

A Dundee court heard of a chap stealing a £50 Ladyshave from Boots. His solicitor said his client had foolishly stolen it as a 'late Mother's Day present'. We pass no comment on the hirsuteness of Dundee women, but we have been told that the women's changing room at the local Lochee Swimming Pool in the town has a sign saying 'No Wet Shaving Please'.

Alleged conversation at Edinburgh Castle between the Princess Royal and Ronnie Browne, the Corrie, beside whom she is seated at a dinner.

The Princess: 'Bother, I've left my speech at the Palace.'

The Corrie: 'Fax it up.'

The Princess: 'It certainly does.'

The heart normally sinks when you hear a joke which begins: 'This duck comes into the pub and orders a pint of lager.' So, this duck comes into the pub and orders a pint of lager. The barman professes astonishment that a duck can talk and drinks lager. The duck explains that she is working on the building site opposite and likes nothing better than a pint at the end of her shift. The duck becomes a regular in the pub. Then a circus comes to town. The ringmaster comes into the pub to put up a poster.

'You'll never guess,' says the barman. 'There is a talking duck comes in here every night. That should amaze your audiences.'

'Tell her to give me a call,' says the ringmaster.

Next night, the duck comes in and the barman tells her about the possible gig. 'A circus?' says the duck. 'With a big canvas tent? What would they want a plasterer for?'

The following debate with our readers ensued:

A duck walks into a bar and says: 'Give us a fish.' The barman explains that it is a pub and he doesn't sell fish. After 10 minutes, the duck returns. 'Any fish?'

'Look, I told you already,' said the barman. 'We don't sell fish. I can give you beer, spirits, wine, cigarettes, crisps, nuts, but I don't sell fish!'

Half-an-hour later the duck is back. 'Go on, give us a fish.' The exasperated barman grabs the duck by the throat and hisses: 'If you come in here again asking for fish, I'll nail your beak to the bar.'

The duck returns a couple of weeks later. 'Do you have any nails?' the duck asks.

'No,' replies the barman.

'Give us a fish then!'

Two ducks are flying over Belfast. One says: 'Quack! Quack!' The other says: 'I'm going as quack as I can.'

Did you hear about the duck that laid a white egg with brown speckles? She said she did it for a lark.

National Chip Week inspired a trawl for appropriate chip shop names: The Batter Merchant, Rutherglen; The Fat Fryer, Blyth, Northumberland; Fat B'stard's, London; Fanny Haddock's Takeaway, Bradford; The Cod Piece, Dorset; Le Codfather, Birmingham.

 **TOM SHIELDS GOES FORTH**

Of course, we prefer the Glasgow varieties such as the Frying Scotsman, Frier Tuck's, and the Merry Frier.

A sailor told us that the emporium of greasy grub adjacent to the Devonport naval dockyard in Plymouth is called Chip Ahoy. A Diary focus group with nothing better to do during National Chip Week came up with On the Batter, Chips That Pass in the Night, A Plaice of Your Own, The Battered Bridie, Cod Bless My Sole, Chipsy Caravan (a Hebridean establishment), and You'll Have Had Your Chips (Edinburgh).

An Ardrossan exile (lucky old exile) tells of a return visit to his home town, and in particular to the Plaza chip shop. He relates: 'The banter was excellent, music to the ears of a local boy now living in Aberdeen. There were two highlights. A youth, having waited in the queue for a good 25 minutes, didn't order fish and chips or even a Killie Pie.

'His order was two pickled onions, two gherkins and a packet of cigarette papers. This prompted a debate about how one would smoke a pickled gherkin and whether or not the boy was old enough to do so legally.

'The shop offers fish suppers for pensioners at a discounted rate.

Every now and then the girl behind the counter was heard to shout above the din, "Salt and vinegar on your fish supper? Salt and vinegar on your Killie Pie supper? Salt and vinegar on your pensioners?" The Plaza's fish and chips are great.'

A LIST OF WHAT WAS IMPORTANT THEN, AND WHAT IS REALITY NOW.

Then: Swallowing acid. Now: Swallowing antacid.
Then: Pothead. Now: Potbelly.
Then: Killer Weed. Now: Weed Killer.
Then: Getting out to a new, hip joint. Now: Getting a new hip joint.
Then: Moving to Spain because it's cool. Now: Moving to Spain because it's warm.
Then: Being called to the headmaster's office. Now: Storming into the headmaster's office.
Then: Getting your head stoned. Now: Getting your headstone.
Then: Long hair. Now: Longing for hair.
Then: Worrying about no one coming to your party. Now: Worrying about no one coming to your funeral.
Then: Trying to look like Marlon Brando or Elizabeth Taylor. Now: Trying not to look like Marlon Brando or Elizabeth Taylor.

Romance is not dead, it seems, in Glasgow's pubs. A young woman was heard to tell the chap who had engaged her in conversation that she 'did not have a romantic bone in her body'. Optimistically, he replied: 'Would you like one?'

We hear of a special constable on one of Scotland's islands, who was called to investigate a car theft from the village hotel one Sunday lunchtime. He was most surprised, as car theft is unknown on the island, nowhere to take the car when the ferry is absent being a primary reason. He was also surprised as he himself had been at the hotel that lunchtime and had seen nothing untoward. Only when he was given a description of the car did a niggling doubt enter his head. So he checked his garage and yes, instead of bringing his wife's car home, he had inadvertently taken the presumed stolen one, which was the same model. A quick handover was arranged, with everyone sworn to secrecy – apart from the person who told the Diary.

Readers familiar with the folklore relating to the characters in the Captain Pugwash cartoon series may find an echo in some of the names involved in the sale of the National Savings Bank at Cowglen, Glasgow. It has been taken over by Siemens Business Services whose top man in the UK is a Mr Pusey. Siemens's address is in Staines Road, Middlesex. There is no truth in the rumour that it is now to be known as the National Sperm Bank.

The scene is the Glasgow office of an English newspaper which has a Scottish edition. A lady executive, who shall remain nameless since we don't actually have an eye-witness account of this one, has been sent up from London to keep the Scots journalists right.

At the daily conference, she listens with interest while the sports editor outlines a proposed feature on the deficiencies of the Scotland football squad. 'Why doesn't Craig Brown go out and buy some new players?' she asks.

It is explained patiently by the sports hack that buying success is not an option for a national team.

'Well,' says the lady executive, with the air of someone who has learned something new and wishes to pass it on to the world, 'I think we should make that clear in the story.'

A teacher is sitting morosely in a hostelry recovering from an unrewarding day at the chalk face. A fellow customer tries to engage him in conversation about his work. 'What is it you teach?' he asks. 'Bastards,' says the teacher, with feeling.

An Ayr man went to the doctor to have something done about the lettuce leaves that were growing from his backside. 'Is it serious?' he asked. 'Yes,' said the doctor, 'I'm afraid it's only the tip of the iceberg.'

Proof that not every Scot is obsessed with money: a survey by Abbey National on people's attitudes to Individual Savings Accounts (ISAs) discovered that when asked, one in five Scots think an ISA is an energy drink.

A Mancunian businessman who has had a fair amount of experience of Glaswegians attended a meeting with some new

business associates in the East End. He went round the meeting and gave everyone there a business card before saying: 'Right, let's get the giggling over with and get on with it.'

The gentleman's name is Perry Balls.

Why is it hard for women to find men who are sensitive, caring and good-looking? An answer might be because those men already have boyfriends. But surely no-one should be as bitter as the woman who said: 'What's the fastest way to a man's heart? Through his chest, with a sharp knife.'

A visitor, returning to Kuwait for the first time since the Gulf War, was impressed by a significant sociological change. On previous visits, she had noted that women customarily walked about 10ft behind their husbands. She observed that the men now walked several yards behind their wives. She approached one of the women for an explanation: 'What enabled women here to achieve this marvellous reversal of roles?'

'Land mines,' replied the Kuwaiti woman.

7. WHAT A STUSHI

We adopted (actually the word is plagiarised) a word game from an American newspaper. The idea is to take a word and add, subtract or change a letter to give it a new meaning. Here are some examples, a few of them a tad American given the source.

Reintarnation: Coming back to life as a hillbilly.

Foreploy: Any misrepresentation about yourself for the purpose of obtaining sex.

Doltergeist: A spirit that decides to haunt somewhere stupid, such as a septic tank.

Sarchasm: The gulf between the author of sarcastic wit and the recipient who doesn't get it.

Coiterie: A very, very close-knit group.

Impotience: Eager anticipation by men awaiting their Viagra prescription.

DIOS: The one true operating system.

Inoculatte: To take coffee intravenously when you are running late.

Hipatitis: Terminal coolness.

Taterfamilias: The head of the Potato Head family.

Osteopornosis: A degenerate disease.

Adulatery: Cheating on your spouse with a much younger person who holds you in awe.

Eunouch: The pain of castration.

Deifenestration: To throw all talk of God out the window.

Karmageddon: It's like, when everybody is sending off all these really bad vibes, right? And then, like, the Earth explodes and it's like a serious bummer.

The Diary and its readers set about discovering some Scottish examples, such as:

Stushi: a fight in a Japanese restaurant.

Clowning: genetic reproduction of people who do not take life very seriously.

Pramraiders: criminals who launch night-time attacks on Mothercare shops.

Rod-rage: the unhappiness of an ageing rock star at his latest alimony hit.

Embrucation: the schooling of Glaswegians in the ways of Auld Reekie. (Malcolm Graham)

Tam O'Shatner: star in movie about alien life forms near Alloway Kirk (Richard Grace).

Episcopalien: occasional visitors to churches in and around Bonnybridge. (Alasdair Noble, Hamilton)

Wishky: wanting to go home with the barmaid after drinking too much. (Colin MacLeod, Thornwood, Glasgow)

Droocot: pigeon loft with a leaky roof.

Corrie doon: take refuge from bad weather in the mountains.

Lad o' paints: male art student.

Tun: derogatory term for a group of exactly 100 Rangers supporters.

Greenpeach: a militant ecological organisation advocating direct action to prevent the genetic modification of fruit.

Overdrift: bank account that seems to run out of money all by itself.

Pottaging: the practice of gay gardeners who hang around sheds hoping to meet other men.

Stoiciou: a philosophical drunk.

Mock Jagger: non-alcoholic beer.

Heidonism: indulging yourself in the practice of the Glasgow kiss.

Parkherd: crowd at a Celtic game.

Fetashism: kinky Greek cheese habit.

Loinlithgow: sexy town in West Lothian.

Nippy Tweetie: bad-tempered canary.

Drabbit: dull and bad-tempered.

Wrabbit: exhausted bunny.

Seilidh: a doon-the-watter concert in the bar of the good ship Waverley.

Kinspeckle: prominent relative.

Larda: Russian car loaded with groceries.

Fleace: an infested sheepskin.

Prontosaurus: fast dinosaur.

Noshtalgia: wistful remembrance of culinary experiences.

Plucre: a person who squeezes spots for financial gain.

Cosy Nostra: a Scottish-Italian criminal group who don't like violence.

Euphorium: feeling of well-being experienced while playing a brass instrument.

Buckfest: cultural event in Coatbridge.

Dievan: small deathbed

Widows '95: computer system for ladies with no e-male.

Tay-Boy: young man from Perth who escorts older women.

Scottosh: cheap souvenirs based on designs of well-known architect.

Anti-semmitic: against the wearing of undershirts.

Hardonica: Washington mouth organ.

Bishoprick: Roddy Wright's former office.

Ibernian: new Spanish striker at Easter Road.

Y2K2 Bug: a mountain to climb for computer programmers.

Improverished: a stand-up comedian short of material.

Scottish Notionalists: those for whom independence is a nice wee idea.

Bravefeart: someone who says 'Ye'll never tak my freedom . . . well, a' right then.'

Timbola: a raffle at Celtic Park.

Smog: kiss from a smoker.

Shaghetti: Italian aphrodisiac.

Scurry: Asian fast food.

Tinnitits: a ringing noise in your breasts.

FFeminism: Women's movement that's really out-front.

Alzimmer's: condition in which you can't remember where you left your walking frame.

Stairfry: barbecue up a close.

Placedo: pill given to hypochondriac tenors.

Legotist: child who refuses to share toys.

Flootball: cultural mix of music and sport in Govan.

Mollyhoddle: to pamper someone, knowing they will suffer for it in the next life.

Oscur: award for best dog actor.

Irrelefant: nothing to do with elephants.

Chews: hielan' Israelites.

Timpetigo: how to spot a Catholic.

Crappielow: semi-derelict football stadium.

The Dairy: newspaper column where anecdotes get milked.

Fellazio: post-match entertainment for Roman footballers.

Me-mail: introspective electronic mail.

Hologran: 3-D picture of granny.

Microsaft: software company based at the Barras. (John Harris, Carluke)

Auntidote: doddery female relative who thinks you're great.

Clartier: famous jeweller's in need of a good wash down.

A ewe for a ewe: retribution, Aberdeen-style.

Irn Brut: your other national aftershave.

Brooze: an injury sustained after rather too many refreshments.

Hagueness: muddled political thinking.

Blairney: flattering political talk.

Essoteric: cheap petrol for select groups in the know.

Genetically moodified: women.

Astrolodger: alien in spare room.

Rustafarian: old Bob Marley fan.

Irn Bra: undergarment made from girders.

Dundee Untied: failure to merge two football teams.

Scrumpet: collective noun for female rugby players.

The Schreme: painting of a housing estate by Edvard Munch.

The Streamie: play about women doing their washing in a burn.

Spqr: roman grocery shop.

Hunburn: result of sunny day at Ibrox.

8. WHAT IF AIRLINES SOLD PAINT?

BUYING PAINT FROM B&Q OR SOME SUCH STORE IS QUITE SIMPLE.

Customer: 'How much is your paint?'

B&Q person: 'We have good quality at £10 a tin and better stuff at £15.'

Customer : 'A tin of the good stuff, please.'

BUT TRY BUYING PAINT FROM AN AIRLINE.

Customer : 'How much is your paint?'

Airline person: 'Well, that depends on a lot of things.'

Customer : 'Then how about giving me an average price?'

Airline person: 'That's too hard a question. The lowest price is £9 a tin but we have 150 different prices, up to £200 a tin.'

Customer : 'What's the difference in the paint?'

Airline person: 'There isn't any difference. It's all the same paint.'

Customer : 'Well, then, I'd like some of that £9 paint.'

Airline person: 'First, I need to ask you a few questions. When do you intend to use it?

Customer: 'I want to paint tomorrow, on my day off'.

Airline person: 'I'm afraid that will have to be the £200 paint.'

Customer : 'When can I get the £9 paint?'

Airline person: 'That would be in three weeks. But you will have to agree to start painting before Friday of that week and continue painting until at least Sunday.'

Customer : 'You've got to be kidding.'

Airline person: 'We don't kid around here. By the way, the price just went up to £12.'

Customer : 'You mean the price went up while we were talking?'

Airline person: 'Yes, we change prices and rules thousands of times a day. Since you haven't actually walked out with your paint yet, I suggest you buy it while the price is still £15. And thanks for painting with our airline.'

A scene at a Nativity play in a Glasgow South Side primary. The little chap cast as the innkeeper had been promoted to Joseph, as the boy originally down for the starring role was off sick. However, the first Joseph recovered before the big dress rehearsal and his stand-in was demoted back to innkeeper. He kept his unhappiness to himself until the dress rehearsal in front of parents. At the point when Mary goes up to the inn, knocks on the door and asks if they can get a room for the night, the innkeeper looked at them both, turned to Mary, and said: 'Aye, you can come in, but he can get to f***.'

This programme of relaxation might come in useful during moments of stress.

Picture yourself near a stream. Birds are chirping in the crisp, cool mountain air. Nothing can bother you here. No one knows this secret place. You are in total seclusion from that place called 'the world'. The soothing sound of a gentle waterfall fills the air with a cascade of serenity. The water is clear. You can easily make out the face of the person whose head you're holding under water.

There now, feeling better?

A scene in the Buchanan Galleries shopping centre in Glasgow. One manager to another at an escalator which is still not moving despite much poking of controls: 'It's no use. We'll need to call the engineer.'

They are interrupted by the archetypal wee Glesga wumman: 'Can ah go up noo, son?'

Management response: 'Aye, missus, but ye'll huv tae walk up manually.'

The scene is the carpet department of a high quality store in Edinburgh. A salesperson, verging on the hoity-toity, is throwing the carpets back and asking if madam (in this case, a wee Edinburgh housewife) likes this one or that one.

Finally, a carpet to the customer's liking is revealed. The housewife says: 'Yes, I can see that in my lounge,' and bends down to touch the carpet. As she does so, she involuntarily passes wind, quite loudly. She is embarrassed and apologises. The salesperson replies: 'Don't worry, madam, when you hear the price you'll shit yourself.'

From Safeway, the people who told us their mince was ideal for recipes, we pass on this eminently sensible serving idea for one of their birthday cakes: 'Suggestions for cutting the cake. Place the cake on a flat surface. Using a long, sharp knife, cut into portions as required.'

An apocryphal story, we hope, from Lanarkshire, where two neighbours have fallen out in a dispute over a boundary wall. Eventually one of them goes to his lawyer. This prompts his neighbour to do likewise, but he inadvertently chooses the same lawyer. The solicitor patiently explains that he cannot act for both, but gives him a letter of recommendation to another lawyer. Although the letter is sealed, the neighbour opens it out of curiosity and reads an account of the dispute with the added paragraph: 'These two are turkeys. You pluck one, and I'll pluck the other.'

The kitchen porter at a Glasgow restaurant was sent to the local supermarket to buy some lychees for the evening sweet menu. Before leaving, he declared that he had never heard of it and was suspicious that his leg was being pulled. On returning, he shouted at the staff: 'I knew you lot were on a wind-up, the wummin at the cheese counter said she'd never heard of it either.'

A blonde, a brunette, a redhead, a vicar, a priest, a rabbi, two giraffes, a duck, a farmer, a lawyer, an accountant, a Mexican, an Indian, a Chinaman, an Irishman, an Englishman, and a Scotsman walk into a bar. The barman says 'Hold on a minute, is this some sort of joke?'.

The following has the demerits of being a poem and is about computer technology. But we include 'The Spell Check' so it can be read by all schoolchildren, except they won't get the point.

> Eye halve a spelling check,
> it came with my pea sea.
> It plainly marques four my revue
> miss steaks eye kin knot sea.
> Eye strike a key and type a word
> and weight four it two say
> Weather eye am wrong oar write,
> it shows me strait a weigh.
> As soon as a mist ache is maid,
> it nose bee fore two long
> And eye can put the error rite,
> its rare lea ever wrong.
> Eye have run this poem threw it,
> Im shore your pleased two no.
> Its letter perfect awl the weigh.
> My checker tolled me sew.

A young man saw an elderly couple sitting down to lunch at McDonald's, Maryhill. He noticed that they had ordered one meal, and an extra cup. As he watched, the gentleman carefully divided the hamburger in half, then counted out the chips, one for him, one for her and so on. Then he poured half of the soft drink into the extra cup and put it in front of his wife.

The old man began to eat and his wife sat watching, with her hands folded in her lap. The young man decided to ask if they would allow him to purchase another meal for them so that they didn't have to split their meagre food. The old gentleman said: 'Oh no. We've been married 50 years, and everything always has and always will be shared, 50/50.' The young man then asked the wife if she was going to eat. She replied: 'Not yet. It's his turn with the teeth.'

Bournemouth Caledonian Society

Founded in 1907 the Society caters for the social requirements of ex patriot Scots and those with Scottish family connections who live in

Pubs being close to many a reader's heart, we pass on the story of an attractive lady going up to the bar in a quiet pub and gesturing alluringly to the barman to come over. When he arrives, she seductively signals that he should bring his face close to hers, and then proceeds to gently caress his full, bushy beard. 'Are you the manager?' she asks, softly stroking his face with both hands. The intrigued barman says no, and she says: 'Can you get him for me? I need to speak to him,' still running her hands up beyond his beard and into his hair.

'I'm afraid I can't,' whispers the aroused barman. 'Is there anything I can do?'

'Yes, there is. I need you to give him this message,' she continues huskily. 'Tell him that there are no towels or toilet paper in the ladies' room.'

At the reception desk of a small hotel, a visitor asks in upper-crust tones for a room. 'Ur you English?' asks the Scot behind the counter.

'Yes, I am.'

'Well, you can beat it. You're no getting a room here.'

The startled Englishman demands to see the manager. The Scotsman then launches into a tirade, shouting: 'I am the manager, you English twit. This is ma hotel, and if I don't want tae hiv you English people staying in ma hotel, that's ma prerogative, pal, so ur ye gonny leave or dae ah hiv tae toss ye oot on yer ear?'

The Englishman leaves. Another guest, overhearing the fracas, asks the manager how he can run a hotel treating potential guests in such a manner. 'To tell you the truth,' replies the Scotsman, 'business isnae doing too good. In fact, if things don't pick up, I'll probably hiv tae move back up tae Scotland.'

The scene is a classroom where the little darlings have been told to search the dictionary for an interesting word around which to construct a sentence. One of the gems produced is: 'My trousers are yearn for me.' The puzzled teacher seeks an explanation. The child opens the dictionary at the appropriate place and says: 'There you are, miss. Yearn – to long for.'

A burglar breaks into a house one night. He is going about his business of shining his torch, identifying valuables and recycling them into his swag-bag. Suddenly a voice cries out: 'Jesus is watching you!' He switches his torch off and stands stock still.

After a few minutes of total silence he gets back down to business, but again is interrupted by: 'Jesus is watching you!'

He shines his torch around and, in the corner of the room, the beam of the torch comes to rest on a parrot.

'Did you say that?' he hisses at the parrot. 'Yes,' the parrot confesses, and squawks: 'I'm just trying to warn you.'

The burglar relaxes. 'Warn me? Who do you think you are anyway?'

'Moses,' replies the bird.

'Moses,' the burglar laughs, 'what sort of idiots would call a parrot Moses?'

'The same kind of people that would name a Rottweiler Jesus,' says the parrot.

A Japanese quine campaigned to undo a slur upon the good name of Govan. Hiroko Macfadyen, a Japanese lady married to a Scot and living happily in Aberdeen, has taken exception to an article in a London-based weekly publication.

The Japanese-language newspaper, the *Eikoku News Digest*, had an item in their agony column in which a young lady, Minako from Richmond, sought advice on her new British boyfriend.

Hiroko Macfadyen sends us this translation of the letter: 'I have a British boyfriend and we are planning to marry. He works for a financial company in the City and he is a polished person. But to tell the truth, he comes from Govan which is a slum in Glasgow, and his family are completely lower class. I am wondering if I will be able to get along well with his family and worry if he will reveal himself one day as lower class.'

Kazuko Hoki, author of the agony column, gave a very full reply which we will have to summarise, pointing out, perspicaciously, that while this Rab C. Nesbitt of the City may not exhibit his lower classness, he will undoubtedly one day exhibit his Scottishness.

He quotes as an example a Scottish person of his acquaintance. 'I have a friend who is chief of an arts centre. He graduated from Cambridge University. He is tall. He speaks posh. He can use a knife and fork properly. But because of the Scottish blood in his family, when he starts drinking he cannot stop singing old Scottish folk songs. This Scot is fond of a party and will not let his guests go home at a decent hour. He keeps on singing and, what's worse, also plays the bagpipes.'

The agony columnist goes on to reassure Miss Minako of Richmond that even though her man is from Govan, all may not be lost. 'He may perhaps reveal himself as lower class by putting too much sugar in his tea,' is as serious as it gets.

The agony person advises that the young Japanese lady learn at least 100 Scottish folk songs so she can sing along with her man.

This panda goes into a restaurant, as they do, and orders a meal. When finished, he gets up, pulls out a gun, shoots the waiter and starts to amble out. The manager, understandably disappointed at the behaviour exhibited, asks for an explanation. The animal shrugs and says: 'I'm a panda. Look it up.'

The manager finds a dictionary, looks up panda, and reads: 'Large bearlike carnivore, native to Asia. Eats shoots and leaves.'

We heard an Australian variation on the panda joke. It relates to guys who get nicknamed wombat, after the animal which eats roots and leaves. But you have to know the local vernacular to fully absorb the implications thereof.

Now for a rarity, a joke or two about engineers.

What's the difference between a mechanical engineer and a civil engineer? Mechanical engineers build weapons. Civil engineers build targets.

Two engineering students, chatting on campus: 'Where did you get such a great bike?' asks the first. The second replies: 'I was walking along yesterday minding my own business when a beautiful woman rode up on this bike. She threw the bike on the ground, tore off all her clothes and said "Take what you want".'

The first nods approvingly: 'Good choice. The clothes probably wouldn't have fitted.'

To the optimist, the glass is half full. To the pessimist, the glass is half empty. To the engineer, the glass is twice as big as it needs to be.

We hear the story of a Glasgow workman called Archie who is given the job of labouring on a building site. The foreman leaves him to dig a trench while he visits another site. On his return a couple of hours later, he is less than impressed with Archie's progress. 'Is that all the dirt you've dug out of the trench?' he asks, to which Archie replies: 'That's all the dirt that was in it.' Archie is now seeking alternative employment.

One of Scotland's ablest after-dinner speakers is Willie Allan, a PE teacher from Fife. He is particularly imaginative when speaking about Methil, his home town, describing it as: 'Beirut in the rain. The only place in Britain where broken biscuits are still legal tender.'

He is not saying the school he teaches in is rough, but the teachers park their cars in a circle.

A reader waded in with the information that a former manager of East Fife, the local football team, once described Methil as the only place he knew where the seagulls flew upside down. This was because there was nothing worth shitting on.

How do the people of Methil install double-glazing? They nail on a second sheet of plywood.

Finally, how do you know you are in Methil? The Kwik-Save trolleys are up on bricks.

The Fife intelligence test: Name a fish that begins with S. Answer: Single.

A snail went into a police station to report that he had been mugged by a turtle. The police officer on duty asked if he could describe the attacker. 'No,' said the snail, 'it happened too fast.'

Another snail joke. A chap slips on a slime trail on his step and, enraged, picks up the offending mollusc and slings it out of sight. A year later, there is a wee knock at the door. The chap answers and the snail looks up and says: 'Right, come on, if you think you're hard enough.'

The scene is the checkout at B&Q, where a customer is stating that he is less than impressed with the disposable barbecue he has purchased. The photo on the lid features a large juicy steak, several fat sausages and a rasher or two of bacon, but when our man opened the barbecue there was no food, just charcoal.

The B&Q assistant explains they are not a food shop, and that the picture was merely an illustration of what might be cooked on the coals. 'Fine, I suppose,' says the customer, 'but I've got another three in the freezer at home.'

CAFE COLON

ENTRADA PUERTA PRINCIPAL

To enhance the quality of the humour in the Diary, we would like to plagiarise Tommy Cooper jokes:

So I went down to my local cafe and said: 'I want to buy an ice cream.'

He said: 'Hundreds and thousands?'

I said: 'We'll start with the one.'

He said: 'Knickerbocker glory?'

I said: 'I do get a certain amount of freedom in these trousers, yes.'

Apparently, one in five people in the world is Chinese. And there are five people in my family, so one of them must be Chinese. It's either my mum or my dad. Or my older brother, Colin. Or my younger brother, Mao Tsetung. But I think it's Colin.

So I went to the dentist. He said 'Say "Aah".'

I said 'Why?'

And he said 'My dog's just died.'

I rang up my local swimming baths. I said: 'Is that the local swimming baths?'

He said 'It depends where you're calling from.'

Some of the benefits of being female that a kindly reader sent in:

Women don't look like a frog in a blender when dancing;

Women can hug a friend without wondering if people think she's gay;

Women don't have to fart to amuse themselves.

An accounting firm in Greenock was looking for an assistant with previous experience in insolvency. A local woman called and asked if the job would suit her husband. Asked about his previous experience, she said he was working in a glue factory.

From Ireland (where else?) an invitation to the 'Grand Official Opening and First Anniversary Celebrations' of the Europa Hotel in Drogheda.

A suggestion to men about to get married: 'Save yourself some time and aggravation – find a woman you don't like and buy her a house.'

Two small boys are swapping football cards. One goes round to his friend's house, but he is not at home. The boy leaves a card at the door. His mother is confused and concerned to overhear this subsequent telephone conversation: 'I came round but you weren't in, so I left Seaman on the doorstep.'

The former Scottish footballer Ian McCall took his new bride on honeymoon to the Spanish resort of Sitges, which also happens to be a mecca for homosexual holidaymakers.

While in Sitges, Mr McCall chose to have his new wife's name tattooed on his arm. She is called Gay.

Graffiti is taken to a pretentious level in Glasgow's fabled West End. A large billboard, advertising Channel 4's *Modern Art* series, had a picture of a large round mirror and the caption: 'Is this art, or just a big wonky mirror?' A local graffitologist added the rejoinder 'or simply clichéd naiveté?'.

A subversive list of children's books:

The Children's Guide to Hitch-hiking
The Boy Who Died From Eating All His Vegetables
Some Kittens Can Fly
The Magic World Inside the Abandoned Refrigerator
Whining, Kicking and Crying to Get Your Way
Things Rich Kids Have, But You Never Will
Controlling the Playground: Respect through Fear
The Care Bears Maul Some Campers and are Shot Dead
Strangers Have the Best Sweets
Your Nightmares are Real

9. ABSOLUTELY AUS-SOME, MATE

JANUARY 2000

A ustralia is the best country in the world. Every other country is merely a holiday destination. This was the response when, before setting off on a trip Down Under, I solicited the opinion of Margaret Moore, a Glasgow woman newly emigrated to those parts. I put the superlative down to the unbounded enthusiasm which Ms Moore has for life, whether it be working for the RAC in rainy old Glasgow or for the Australian Automobile Association in sunny Adelaide. After three weeks in Oz, I had to concede that Margaret is not too far off the mark.

My preconceptions of Australia naturally came from TV and film and encounters with those Bruces and Sheilas returned to the Old World with their amusing and direct figures of speech. Australia was *Neighbours* and *Skippy*. Australia was a vast and hostile terrain. (The film *Walkabout*, with poor Jenny Agutter wandering the Outback in her school uniform, sticks in the mind for some reason.) Australia was a country culturally marooned somewhere between Britain and the US. With the zeal of the convert, I now testify that Australia is

BRUCE & STIFF
FUNERAL HOME

the country of the new millennium. It is young, vibrant, cosmopolitan and the 17 million inhabitants are lucky bastards (sorry, the odd swear word used for emphasis is perfectly acceptable) to be living there. In short, I quite liked it Down Under.

The reason for the visit was to investigate the psyche of the Australian nation as it went to the polls in the referendum on becoming a republic or retaining the monarchy. With consummate timing, I missed the referendum by two weeks. It was a damp squib anyway, with the Aussies voting 54 per cent for the status quo, despite the best efforts of such republican campaigners as Eddie McGuire, who can best be described as Australia's Des Lynham.

Eddie is a boy with roots in Glasgow's tough Garthamlock scheme, who has achieved fame and fortune fronting Australia's most popular TV sports show, which is saying something in a country where sport is king. It is called *The Footie Show* (Aussie Rules footie, not our footie). Eddie bought his own football club in Melbourne and is forever being mentioned in the gossip columns. His republicanism is allied to a devotion to Celtic, which he inherited from his Glasgow father. During his analysis of Aussie footie on his TV show, he manages to insert the odd reference to the bhoys in green and white.

Eddie McGuire and his fellow republicans lost primarily because their opponents, led by federal prime minister John Howard, cleverly manipulated the question. The alternative to the dear old Queen as head of state would be a politician not elected by popular vote, but nominated by other politicians. This was an option many would-be anti-monarchists found unacceptable.

I could detect no great passion for the monarchy among the people I spoke to, apart from a lady in Cairns who just loved the Queen Mother. But then her other great enthusiasm for things British was wallpaper 'with big floral patterns and those neat little borders'. In truth, the issue of monarchy versus republic did not seem to impinge too much on the consciousness of most modern Australians, who seemed too busy just getting on with life. With no great constitutional issue to dissect, your reporter Down Under turned his attention to analysing how they live this life.

The great thing about the Aussies is they do not live to work. Once the day's drag is done, they devote themselves to leisure. It is an exhilarating regime of sun, sea, sand, Chardonnay and seafood

allied to the pursuit of healthy exercise. The blue skies and warm weather are positive inducements to sporting activity in the great outdoors. Diving, snorkelling, surfing, swimming, running, walking, climbing and a host of other sports are on hand. Unfortunately, a doctor's line prevented me from taking part in most of these energetic pursuits but I spoke to people who do.

A good example is Brian McNulty, a young Glaswegian living in Sydney. Brian works as a merchant banker. For two weeks solid he works nightshift, prowling the American financial markets. The third week he spends down the coast, up the Blue Mountains, or deep in a rainforest somewhere. 'It's great exercise and, even in these remoter locations, there is usually a party going on,' he says. Young Mr McNulty has quite taken to Australian life.

In Melbourne, I found Gaynor Hall, another recent Scots emigrant working for a law firm. She is no stranger to the busy social life which Melbourne has, but, almost to her own surprise, she finds herself of a weekend taking part in competitive events with her workmates which involve running, swimming, canoeing and biking.

A common sight in all of the Australian seaside locations are the kids pedalling off to the beach after school, surfboard on the handlebars. If it's not surfing or swimming, it's a spot of soccer, cricket, footie, rugby or tennis. It is little wonder that Australia is currently world leader in a whole host of sports.

Despite my doctor's line, I was determined to dip my toe into some of the delights of the Australian great outdoors. I failed the medical for my first attempt at scuba diving on the Great Barrier Reef because of an ear operation some years ago and abandoned the expedition, much to my chagrin since I was being accompanied hand-in-hand by Eske, an instructress for whom the words 'Polynesian' and 'babe' are totally insufficient.

When I went snorkelling, I had also had a bit of trouble as my mask kept filling up with water. The problem was solved by Bert, a less comely instructor, who approached me with a tub of Vaseline. The Vaseline, thankfully, was to be smeared liberally on my hirsute upper lip to provide a seal between mask and facial hair. It worked, and spurning Bert's kind offer to hold my hand (by this time Eske was off guiding another lucky old codger), I went for a solo float over the coral reef. The plan was to stay in the water for five minutes

just to say I had done it. An hour later I was still flippering about, absorbed by the multicoloured fish, none of which, luckily, were sharks. It was just sublime, and a rare treat for the other tourists to catch a glimpse of that unusual species, the Great White Scottish Whale.

While in tropical North Queensland, I nearly went for a walk in the Daintree Park rainforest. I was up for it, even though in Scotland I normally eschew country walks for fear of meeting dangerous wildlife such as rabbits. I was even dressed for the occasion in a pair of khaki trousers with 12 pockets, a matching shirt with another 12 pockets and a bush hat. It was slightly embarrassing to note that many of the other tourists in the car park were wearing Union Jack shorts and Hard Croc Cafe T-shirts. It was even more embarrassing when some of them, taking me for a rainforest ranger, asked advice on the various walking routes.

I must have got at least 100 yards down the jungle trail before I was made more than slightly nervous by rustling noises from the undergrowth. It might very well have been the chap in the Union Jack shorts and Hard Croc Cafe T-shirt, but it could also have been a form of wildlife I had no desire to encounter. A sign at the car park said that if we were lucky, we would come across some giant dragon lizards. This big feartie retreated to the safety of the car and the drive to view the nearby 'mighty Barron Falls'.

The terrain surrounding the falls was indeed mighty, on a scale with the Victoria Falls in Africa, but there was something missing: water. A nearby notice explained: 'When the Djabugay people were the only inhabitants of this area, these falls were a spectacular sight for most of the year. Most of the water is now used for hydro-electric power and the falls are only in full flow during heavy rains.' It is an irony of eco-tourism that the mighty Barron Falls have been switched off to provide electricity for the hotels, bars and restaurants for the many visitors who make their way to tropical North Queensland to see such glories as the Falls.

Observant readers may have spotted in the author a hint of antipathy towards nature in the raw, and eco-tourism in general. For me, the glories of Australia lay in its great twin cities of Sydney and Melbourne. These metropoles spend much effort and money rivalling one another. I would not compare them with each other. Any comparison should be with the other great cities of the world,

and both Melbourne and Sydney would come high on my list of favourites, something to do with the brilliance of that antipodean sky and the regular possibility of a bit of sun. But it has more to do with the people. They have come from many other countries and cultures, and have brought much that is good with them to their new land. Let us start with the most important cosmopolitan influence – the food.

Australia is not so much a melting pot as a cooking pot. It is a land of abundant fresh food and cooks of many cuisines. Sue Williams, an eminent Australian journalist, embarked on a series of weekly articles, a trawl of Sydney's restaurants called 'Around the World in 80 Meals'. She found enough diversity to achieve the 80. Inevitably, the English cafe involved was a low point.

The Aussie cliche 'throw another prawn on the barbie' became a delicious reality for me. Upon arrival in Sydney, I embarked upon a crustacean overdose. The first four meals were all prawn-centred. To start with, some spicy chaps for dinner in Pho Pasteur, a Vietnamese cafe favoured by students. Breakfast next day was at the Sydney fishmarket restaurant. Despite the attraction of such delicacies as red snapper fillets on toast, my choice was barbecued prawns. Dinner was garlic prawns in an Aussie-Spanish restaurant. I was heading for a traditional breakfast next day, honest, when I came across a fish shop in Kings Cross which will deep-fry your purchases there and then. The prawns in their wee breadcrumb overcoats were too much to resist.

In Melbourne, the prawn was replaced by quail as the leitmotif. Tender, deep-fried quail in a chilli marinade, in a Chinese restaurant. And a quail supper in a Greek 24-hour cafe. Not too many quail, please, I joked, but it comes as standard, two birds and a big pile of chips.

Other Aussie culinary highlights included enjoying a giant T-bone steak with everything, available almost anywhere for about £6, and being a bit of a voyeur in a restaurant in Cairns as two lesbian lovers enjoyed a romantic meal of a two-litre jug of Bloody Mary and two dozen oysters. They were a bit riotous, but did not offend the restaurant code of conduct which was, according to the sign, 'No bare chests. Unruly behaviour or swearing will not be tolerated'.

Melbourne and Sydney are party cities. Australia used to be famous for its bizarre licensing laws when the pubs were closed at 6 p.m., and the ensuing 'six o'clock swill', when thirsty punters got

as drunk as they could, was a national disgrace. This has been replaced by a cool culture, with some bars open 24 hours and clubs that are still admitting customers at 10 a.m. I was allowed into one such haven of loud music by a kindly if bemused bouncer, while on a post-prandial stroll in Melbourne. It was full of young people drinking bottles of water and not having conversations. I couldn't see the point, made an excuse, and left.

One preconception I had carried to Australia was that the local beer would be fizzy and tasteless. The truth is that Australia's favourite beer, Victoria Bitter, is a delightful drop and cheap at just over £1 a pint. It is on a par with, and probably just a bit better than, Glasgow's beloved Tennents lager. I confess that some moments of my Aussie euphoria may have been fuelled by the VB, as locals call it.

After a night on the VB and the prawns, it is time to avail oneself of an aspect of the oriental lifestyle which has been imported to Australia by the Korean community. I was introduced to the delights of the Korean bath house by Jimmy Thomson, a former *Herald* journalist and now a TV luvvie in Australia (well, as luvvie as a boy from Dumfries can be). The bath house is situated in the Capital Hotel in King's Cross. King's Cross is the red light area in a city where a substantial industry has grown up involving Asian girls and quantities of body oil. But the Korean bath house is squeaky clean. You can loll about in the luxury of the ginseng bath, the spa, or the very hot and the very cold pools. 'Prepare to be steamed, scrubbed and soaked within an inch of your life,' the guide book says.

The bath house has separate sections for men and women, so nakedness is the norm. A bit embarrassing, this, so when your correspondent was handed a piece of cloth the size of a tea towel, it came in handy for draping decorously in front of the dangly bits. Even more embarrassing was walking into the bath house to see everyone else wearing the tea towel, bandana-style, on their heads. With an inward cry of 'banzai!', your reporter plunged into the bath house culture.

Even to the extent of undergoing the skin scrub. It is quite simple. You put your life in the hands of a masseur whose skill lies in attacking you with what feels like a wire-wool chamois. It is a particularly challenging experience, especially when the exfoliation implement is wheeched awfully close to the delicate scrotal area.

There then follows a vigorous rub-down with a hot soapy towel, and a hose-down with a powerful shower. Invigorating isn't in it. You will know that you have been chamoised.

One of the scars which disfigures the otherwise acceptable countenance of Australia is racism. There are some Australians, mainly the older people of British origin but some younger and from other European roots, who ritually verbally abuse those they perceive as black, or brown, or yellow, or just not like them. They use such words as darkie, slopehead and bludger. Bludger is Aussie slang for a lazy person. It would be funny, were it not so sad, to hear some of the 'white' Australians characterise the Asian Australians as bludgers. The Chinese, Pakistanis, Koreans and others of Far Eastern origin tend, of course, to be among the hardest-working and best-educated in the land. (Pause for politically incorrect joke. How do you know that you have been burgled by a Vietnamese? Your dog has disappeared and someone has done all your children's homework.)

The worst vituperation is reserved for the Aborigines. The new Australians stole their land, embarked upon genocide and stole the souls of those who survived. They introduced the Aborigines to strong drink and nicotine, and now wonder why they fecklessly hang around street corners bevvying instead of getting a decent job and a house. Many Australians will recite how the 'abo bludgers', a mere 500,000 out of a population of 17 million, use up two-thirds of the social security budget. One chap I encountered in a small town in Queensland took his argument further: he would give them as much money as they wanted in the hope that they would drink and smoke themselves to death all the sooner. His comments were a bit of a conversation-stopper.

All I could think of saying was: 'So, how many years ago did you leave Fife to come to Australia?'

Being a bleeding-heart liberal in these matters I made a wee effort to get to know something about Aboriginal culture, albeit in a kind of Disneyfied setting. It was the Wildworld animal park near Cairns. One of the daily features is a half-hour talk by an Aboriginal girl called Kasia. She explains how amazingly environmentally friendly the Aborigine way of life was, and how clever they were at foraging for food. They had ways of catching fish undreamt of by the Vale of Leven's poacher lads. It was a fascinating civilisation, now scattered

 **TOM SHIELDS GOES FORTH** 97

to reservations and city slums. So what is life like for the Aborigine in Australia today? Kasia felt she wasn't really qualified to say. With her job, her flat in town and her $25,000 car, she is not entirely typical.

My other encounter with Aboriginal people was not entirely anthropological. Fleeing an Irish pub full of English tourists in a Cairns shopping mall, I met a group of Aborigines sitting on a bench. I sat down and they offered me a slug of the bottle of cheap port they were passing around. I asked a few questions about life in their township, down the coast from Cairns. They were polite but more interested in where they could get another bottle of port and some cigarettes. The bottle shop was closed but I managed to get some port from a nearby hotel, which didn't have the cheap £3 variety, so a bottle of vintage £20 stuff ended up being handed around. I had no cigarettes, but my Cohiba cigar from Cuba found favour as it was communally puffed upon. Typical bleeding-heart liberal. All I had achieved was to give them a taste for brands of alcohol and nicotine they could not afford.

The most important discovery during my little Cook's tour of Australia and its people was how open they are. The Aussies love to talk. The waitress at breakfast who asks how you are doing is actually interested. The bus driver will chat amiably while a confused tourist rakes through a pile of coins to find the correct fare. Some mornings it took 20 minutes to buy my morning paper from the newsagent across from the hotel as the proprietor sustained a conversation about matters of great import, and of no import at all.

The laid-back Australian way of life is epitomised by a refrain which appears to be constantly on their lips: 'no worries'. I think it's the prawns and the VB that makes them so cheerful. Or it could be the sun. Or living in a young country with a special quality of life. The only things wrong with Oz are that it's too far away, and I am not rich enough or young enough to bridge the gap.

10. CHICKEN OR EGG

There's this really sexy chicken and a very fanciable egg. They end up in bed together. Afterwards the chicken leans back on the pillow, lights a languid cigarette, and says: 'Well, that answers that question.'

The scene: the swimming pool at a tourist complex in Lanzarote. A Scottish couple have made friends, as you do, with some people from Yorkshire.

One of the subjects of conversation, over a drink or two, is the irritating German habit of putting towels on the best loungers at the poolside. After a particularly convivial late-night session verging on the early morning, the Scotsman decides that he will outdo the Germans, and before retiring at 4 a.m. he places towels on two sunbeds in prime locations.

Next morning, he arrives at the poolside to find two Germans ensconced on the chairs. The Scotsman launches into a tirade, stopping just short of mentioning the war and the German proclivity for invading other people's territory. The Germans profess no knowledge of any towels. Our man is eventually dragged away by his peace-loving wife and is not allowed to return to the debate when their son reports that their towels are lying at the bottom of

the pool. The Scots are joined by the chap from Yorkshire who gleefully and conspiratorially informs them that he had exacted some revenge by nipping down at 6 a.m. and chucking a couple of the Germans' towels into the pool.

The scene: a municipal skip kindly provided for the citizens of Hamilton by that nice South Lanarkshire council. There is security at the cleansing depot to deter midgie rakers, but it was not in evidence on this occasion.

When our environmentally aware correspondent slings the first of the gleanings of his cleaned-up garage into the nearest skip, there is a yell from inside as an unofficial recycler makes his presence known. Our man then hears the ringing of a mobile phone and a one-sided conversation from the skip, which goes: 'What?' Then, in increasingly impatient tones: 'No, no, no, no, no,' concluding with: 'I'm busy. I've told you not to call me here.'

Back in the world of blindingly obvious statements, a sign in an East Kilbride library informs us: 'These books may be borrowed.'

The Diary's Morals Correspondent witnessed an interesting scene during the departure of the Tall Ships from Greenock. He says: 'I was on the Esplanade, the place was absolutely mobbed, I was standing beside three teenage girls. As the Russian ship went past, a magnificent sight with about a hundred Russians in the rigging, one of the girls yelled: "Haw Ivan, whit are we gonny call the wean?"'

Instructions on a packet of 2ft long garden flares: 'Do not swallow.' Perhaps the safety hint is aimed at a minority group, such as circus performers.

Amid mail bags of congratulatory letters to George Robertson on his post as Lord Robertson of Nato was one which read (more or less): 'Dear Robertson, I cannot stand you. I think you are bloody useless with your tiny wee mouth and the way your wig doesn't fit . . .'
George's reply was (more or less): 'Thank you for your letter but do you think I would have a bought a wig with a hole in the top?'

The BBC remains a bastion of the English language as she should be spoke. As such, the corporation has strict standards on words which may or may not be used. Two memos, or 'editorial compliance reminders' as they are called, recently came our way.

The first is headed 'Welshing' and states: 'The BBC's Programme Complaints Unit has upheld complaints about the inclusion of the expression 'welshing'. It is usually used to describe reneging on an agreement, but it is also considered by some Welsh people to be offensive ... Further use would be difficult to defend.'

The second deals with 'Twat, Use of Word'. It begins: 'There is some uncertainty about the meaning of the word "twat" and, therefore, about attitudes towards its suitability for inclusion in our programmes. In many parts of the country it is another term for the C word and has the same capacity to offend.' The BBC's adjudication is: 'It is not acceptable pre-watershed on television or on radio at times when children are likely to be in the audience.' Which rules out the script we have been working on for a situation comedy, working title *Welshing Twat*.

Pollok Golf Club on the south side of Glasgow is one of the sport's more expensive and exclusive establishments. There are some residents of the nearby working-class barrios who do not have the cash or the cachet to obtain membership but who still enjoy the splendid courses. They do so by nipping out of the woods adjacent to the third hole and taking advantage of any slack in the golfing traffic. They usually manage a reasonable round before disappearing back into the woods on or around the 16th hole.

So popular is this cheap and healthy pursuit that the indocumentados of Pollok even have their own championship. We are told that the final of this unofficial competition took place recently, complete with a gallery following the two participants. Being a final, play was somewhat slower than usual and a party of legal, fully paid-up members caught up with them and asked if they could play through. The reply was a blunt refusal, along the lines of: 'F*** off, pal, this is a competition.'

Scene: a pub next to Dumbarton Central station. For some inexplicable reason, two comely German girls have chosen to alight at this station and seek refreshment in the bar. The denizens of the establishment, unused to visits by tourists, especially comely foreign burds, take an immediate interest. The language barrier proves insuperable as various chat-up lines wither on the vine. One Dumbarton Lothario decides that sign language is the answer and does a piece of mime. He points to himself. He lays his head on his hands. He points to the German girl who is the object of his courtship. Then he takes his bunnet from his head and lets it fall to the floor.

Having failed with this approach, he returns to his pals, who ask him what he had been on about. They got the bit about 'I sleep with you', but could not see the significance of the bunnet. 'I was trying to tell her I would sleep with her at the drop of a hat,' explained the unsuccessful swain.

A Playstation game called *Total Soccer* is brought to our attention. It's not a bad wee game, but because of copyright law the makers were unable to use the names of real football teams. They got round this problem by changing one letter in the name of the team, for example 'Fanchester United'. The deplorable sectarianism in Scottish football could spread south of the Border when 'Hunderland' play 'Timbledon'. Still on the subject of religion, we could have 'Greenock Mormon'. Other teams might include: 'Queer of the South' or 'Queer's Park'. 'Clype' would be the kind of team always complaining to the referee. 'Fearts' sound like a bunch of cissies. 'Liverpooh', 'Blackpooh', and 'Hartlepooh' would leave themselves open to accusations of execrable performances. Other suggestions were welcomed, apart from any involving Huntly.

The Barras held a farmers' market at the weekend where folk from the country could sell their produce direct to the customer. A local citizen spied an old pal wandering around the stalls and asked him what he was up to.

'Oh, I'm just in for a gander,' he replied.

His friend looked dubious. 'I've not seen anyone selling them.'

An Antipodean reader was confused by the *Herald*'s sports page description of Aberdeen being 'rooted' at the foot of the Premier League. 'Root' is an Aussie variation of the F-word.

This reminded the Diary of an Aussie joke; a Queensland farmer told his mate that he intended driving down to Sydney for a short break. When his mate asked which route he was taking, he replied: 'I think I'll just take the wife. She stood by me during the drought.'

With the Scottish National Party employing a whole squad of researchers and secretaries for its members of the Scottish Parliament, it was decided that a staff association should be set up. The new staff were issued with a survey on how such an association should be formed and what its priorities should be.

One anonymous response suggested names for the new organisation: Association of SNP Staff Working In Parliament Etc; Organisation Representing General and Staff Matters; and General Union for Staff Socialising, Entertainment, and Training.

The ends to which people will go in the search for chronic acronyms. (To save you the bother, they are Asswipe, Orgasm, and Gusset.)

The normally mild-mannered Murdo MacLeod covers the parliament for the BBC's Gaelic service, *Radio Nan Gaidheal*. He proffered his business card to a young lady at the parliament, who squealed with delight and said: 'That's marvellous. You have a Gaelic version typed on the back.'

'No, madam, the Gaelic version is on the front,' he declared. Missing his defensive tone, she ploughed on: 'The word *poilitigeach* for politics. Is that just an English word turned into Gaelic?'

'No,' he again corrected her. 'It is a Greek word turned into Gaelic.' And with the score at 2–0 to the Gaels, he quietly walked away.

A sign of the hard times prevailing in the farming trade: a farmer wins £5 million in the lottery. 'What are you going to do with the money?' he is asked. 'I suppose I'll just keep farming until it's all gone,' he replies.

In the odd moment of recreation between making the many fantastic movies and TV series currently in production, Scottish film folk amuse themselves by coming up with Scottish versions of film classics:

Dumb and Dumbarton
Getting Leven
Aberlady and the Tramp
Silence of the Glamis
Clackmannan the Iron Mask
The Killin Fields
Forfar the Madding Crowd

The Diary and its readers concocted the following:

Brechin Counter
101 Dalmellingtons
Cleopatna
Tainspotting
Beauly & the Beast
The Tullibody Snatchers
Journey to the Centre of Perth
Wick up Your Ears

Ordinary Peebles
Balerno with Bo Derek
Clynderella
You Only Live Dyce
Dial M for Milngavie
It's a Wonderful Fife
Kelty's Heroes
Cat Ballingry

Leven, on a Jet Plane
The Madness of Kingussie
Croy, the Beloved Country
A Fistful of Dollar
The man Who Came in from the Coldstream
Lock, Stock and Two Smoking Barras
The Ziegfeld Forres of 1923
Full Methil Jacket
All Quiet in the Western Baths
Every Which Way But Lewis
Murders in the Rhu Morgue
Forres Gump
Clynder's List
Sheepless in Newbattle
Doctor at Largs
Buckfast at Tiffany's
Gunfight at the Bookie Coral

Renfrew Over the Cuckoo's Nest
When Harris Met Sanday
Driving Ruchazie
They Died With Their Butes On
But and Ben Hur
Play Menstrie For Me
The Man From Bonkle
Saving Loch Ryan
Saturday Night Peever
Last Mango in Harris
Midden Night Cowboy
Tie Me Up, Tie Me Dowanhill
Bar Trek
Things to do in Denny When You're Dead
Planet of the Papes
Mission Nae Bother At All

A very bad joke favoured by Scottish football fans abroad. The perfect location for this play on wurdz is the baggage reclaim of an airport. The perfect victim is a comely lady, who is approached as she stands gazing at the luggage carousel and asked in a 'where's the burdz' manner: 'Looking for your holdall?'

Elaine C. Smith on playing the character of a male handyman in her TV series: 'The hardest bit was creating his beer belly. Well actually it wasn't that hard, I just took my bra off.'

A classroom tale. A wee chap, not at all overawed by his first day at school, enters the dinner hall in the company of a new pal. He approaches the dinner lady and asks for 'a table for two, please'.

A Scots tourist, just back from a holiday in Florida before the hurricanes arrive, is heard to tell his mate: 'Dolphins really are intelligent. After a few weeks of captivity, they can train Americans to stand at the edge of a pool and throw them fish.'

 **TOM SHIELDS GOES FORTH** 105

The old saying that in Kilwinning they eat their young appears to be given credence by a course offered by the community education department of North Ayrshire Council. Under 'What's On – Kilwinning Area', the good folk of Ayrshire's Burgh of Culture are invited to come along to the Blacklands Hall and sign up for 'Family Cooking (Bring Your Child)'.

We are entirely prepared to believe this story of a member of the crew of an American airline who arrived at Glasgow and, being unfamiliar with the layout of the airport, asked for directions. What she actually said was: 'Excuse me, where do I interface with the ground transportation unit?' After a rapid piece of translation, the airport staff member replied: 'Adjacent to the anterior portal, miss.'

Attendance at each and every session of the Scottish Parliament is not compulsory. But registering your vote is always a good idea. Gordon Jackson QC, MSP for Govan, has been given a nickname by the SNP. It is allegedly a reference to his turning up at the last minute to vote. He is called Crackerjack, after the famous TV programme which began: 'It's five to five . . . time for Crackerjack!'

The debate over whether fox-hunting should be banned in Scotland reminded an Ayr reader of a public meeting in a run-down council housing scheme, where the local councillor was pledging all sorts of improvements sometime in the future. He was asked about rats. The councillor pledged that if they were a problem then the council would trap or poison them until they were eliminated.

'What about the foxes?' asked another tenant. Just as boldly the councillor said they would be dealt with in exactly the same way, and he was surprised and delighted at the loud cheer he received. Only when the meeting ended did his local housing official tell him that the Foxes were a well-known anti-social family living locally.

An apocryphal tale from an international women's conference, at which the subject for discussion was how to empower women in the home.

The first speaker was the British representative. She stood up and said: 'I decided to make a stand against my husband's oppression, so I told him that I would no longer be doing the washing. After the first day I saw no result; after the second day I saw nothing; but on the third day he did his own washing.' The delegates applauded this brave stand for women's rights.

The second speaker was from America. She stood up and said: 'I told my husband that I was no longer prepared to cook for him as it was a form of enslavement. After the first day I saw no result; after the second day I saw no result; but on the third day he cooked dinner for both of us.' Again the conference applauded.

Next came the Australian delegate. She said: 'I told my husband that I would no longer be doing the shopping. After the first day I saw nothing; after the second day I saw nothing; but on the third day I could see a little bit out of my left eye.'

They are a strict bunch at the Pensions Appeals Tribunal for Scotland. A copy of a judgment arrived at our desk. It gives the name of the claimant, which includes the details 'deceased' in brackets. It then declares that the case has been adjourned and gives the reason: 'Claimant failed to attend.'

A touch of real life as it is lived in Possilpark, the drug-blighted arrondissement of Glasgow. Our story involves a lady from the

area whose only personal contact with drugs is smoking many packets of cigarettes every day. At the age of 88 she says: 'Ah don't think these fags are doin' me any good.' But our sad story is that a local young man had reached such a state of despair with his drug addiction that he was found dead, hanging from a balcony. After the lying-in for the deceased, with a decade or two of the rosary, the talk among the local women turned to how the world in general and Possil in particular had been brought so low, and what could be done to rid the area of the scourge of drugs. 'Well,' opined the heroine of our tale, 'I'd bring back hanging for a start.'

Spotted, the following written on the filthy back door of a white Transit van on Loch Lomondside: 'John Clark & Sons, international plumbers. London, Paris, New York, and Oban. (Mainly Oban).'

Dept of We Hope We Know What They Mean. BBC *Wildlife* magazine lists bird-spotting attractions, including the Farm Islands in Northumbria where, they say, 'More than 19 species of seabirds including puffins, guillemots and terns breed here in their thousands. One of the few places you can get so close to a shag you can smell it.'

We are talking cormorants here, of course.

Stuck to a window of a telephone box in Plockton, a BT sign with an illustration of a telephone and the words: 'You may telephone from here.'

We hear of a visit to Palestine by the comrades of the STUC, led by General Secretary Campbell Christie. Oor Campbell is discussing matters of mutual interest with Palestinian trade union leaders. One of their problems, it seems, is the scattered nature of the workforce. 'It must be hard for you to collect your dues,' Campbell says. There is a stunned silence before the Palestinians realise that Campbell is talking about subscriptions and not their near but unloved neighbours, the Jews.

A young lady driver was pulled in by the traffic polis one morning when visibility was very poor. 'What does the Highway Code tell us to do when we see mist or fog?' the cop asked in an avuncular but firm manner. Puzzled but keen to cooperate, the young lady thought for a minute before giving this reply, worthy of the Tufty Club: 'We should put on Mister Lights.'

And now a light-hearted tale from the Northern Ireland marching season. A child in the Ormeau Road finds a sash lying in the street and takes it home to put in the bin. His mother tells him that they don't want such a thing in their rubbish and suggests he put it in the litter bin out in the street. He is doing so when his father says not to sully the area with such an item and to take it to the skip three streets away. The boy is walking with the sash when he meets his grandfather. He explains where he is going to dump it.

That's not far enough, says grandad, who suggests he take it all the way to the city dump. The wee boy, exasperated, says: 'I've only been an Orangeman ten minutes and I've been re-routed three times already.'

English, as she is translated from foreign tongues:
From a brochure of a car rental firm in Tokyo: 'When passenger of foot heave in sight, tootle the horn. Trumpet him melodiously at first, but if he still obstacles your passage then tootle him with vigour.'

On the door of a Moscow hotel room: 'If this is your first visit to Russia, you are welcome to it.'

Sign in the office of a Roman doctor: 'Specialist in women and other diseases.'

Three Free Kirk ministers are killed in a plane crash. They go to the Pearly Gates and knock.

'Who's there?' St Peter shouts.

'Three Wee Free ministers,' they reply.

'Well,' says the Keeper of the Keys, 'you can come in if you want, but you'll no like it.'

A question from North Lanarkshire Council territory, where the various geographical power groups are still skirmishing: how many Motherwell councillors does it take to close down a project in Coatbridge?

As many as are in the country at the time.

A tale of a postman who has to deliver a registered letter. His knock on the door is answered by a lad of no more than 12 years old. In one hand he has a can of beer, in the other a cigarette. In the near distance, up the lobby, the postman discerns the form of a young lady in a state of undress. 'Is your mum or dad in, son?' the postie asks.

'What do you think?' the lad replies.

The medical press throws up some interesting and unusual information. A study of 'the mechanisms of nausea and vomiting' in the *Journal of the Royal Naval Medical Service* contains the statement: 'The spectrum of problems that give rise to vomiting is very wide, ranging from normal pregnancy to the bizarre psychological aberration of erotic vomiting at each other.' Which might explain the cries of 'Hughie! Hughie!' to be heard in back closes the length and breadth of Scotland.

11. SCOTLAND RULES

SYDNEY, 18 NOVEMBER 1999

It was an undignified scramble for tickets to see the action between England and Scotland. This wasn't Wembley, but a whole world away, in Sydney. Unlike much of the rest of the world, the Auld Enemy match was not widely available on TV as the rights for the Euro 2000 play-off double-header were bought by Setanta, a small satellite company who sold the coverage on to a limited number of pubs and clubs.

Demand far exceeded supply, and for every one exiled Scot who managed to find a place where he could pay his $20 entry fee, there were three or four turned away at the door. The biggest Sydney venue to show the Hampden and Wembley games was the Aussie Rules Club. This is a supporters' venue run by the governing body of the Australian sport, a combination of rugby, soccer and unarmed combat. The Scottish equivalent of the Aussie Rules Club would be if the SFA had opened a massive social club in Glasgow where the likes of Ernie Walker and Jim Farry would be found mingling with the fans.

With a time difference of 11 hours, the Aussie Rules Club put on a double bill of televised football. Doors opened at 3 a.m. with the

Turkey-Ireland game kicking off first, followed by the Wembley encounter at 7 a.m.

It was a case of first come, first served. Luckily the King's Cross area of Sydney, where the Aussie Rules Club is located, is on the lively side, with pubs and clubs open all hours.

Unfortunately, most of the clubs are establishments offering entertainment of a carnal nature and the fan in search of football has to run the gamut of hucksters and hookers.

Many of the latter are six-foot tall, muscular and intimidating, and wear short mini-dresses, not unlike many of the Tartan Army.

It was Ireland's turn first to act out their tragedy, going out on the away-goals rule. It was even more of a tragedy for the Irish fans watching at the Aussie Rules Club. With three minutes to go and Ireland pressing for the vital goal, a satellite technician somewhere pulled a switch and the picture changed from the Irish charge in Istanbul to England fans warming up at Wembley. There were howls of derision and a few cans thrown at the big screen as another chapter was written in England's oppression of Ireland.

For the Scotland match, the club's 500-seater big-screen arena was a microcosm of Wembley, with Scots and English delivering cheerful comments to each other.

As is normal in battles with the Auld Enemy, the disaffected Irish were on our side.

There was ritual anthem abuse, just like in the stadium, before the fans settled down for the ebb and flow of the game.

Our Braveheart showed the usual occasional frailty, prompting Jimmy Thomson, late of Dumfries but now a TV mover and shaker in Sydney, to comment: 'I see they've got Paul Scholes man-marking Hendry again, waiting for an opening in our penalty area.'

But soon the unlikely-looking Scottish line-up began to do the business and the English fans went quiet. 'You're supposed to be at home,' the Scots-Irish chanted, aware of the irony of the 12,000-mile distance from Wembley. It was eerie and quite moving to hear the Tartan Army in Wembley echoed by their fellow countrymen at the other side of the world. The Aussies, who are no slouches when it comes to verbalising their feelings about sport, appeared impressed by the noise. Don Hutchison's goal spurred our antipodean fans on to louder efforts. It seemed we might turn the English fans' Great Escape metaphor back on them.

Would Scotland equalise? Would Kevin Keegan put on a jacket with an even bigger neck and hide all of his face? Would it go to extra time, leaving the Sydney diaspora to find an excuse as to why they were going to be late at the office? The Scotland team were doing it again to their fans. There is nothing worse than that faint glimmer of hope.

There is also nothing worse than that man Seaman between the English posts. He conspired, yet again, to deny us the vital goal. Seaman is supposed to be heading beyond his sell-by date these days, but he still managed to throw his hands out and stop the Christian Dailly header which could have sent us to the Euro 2000 finals.

For Scotland, it was another magnificent failure by the narrowest of margins. At full-time, as we poured out on to the streets of King's Cross, Sydney, it was 9 a.m. 'We're supposed to be at work,' a Scottish fan sang.

The ladies in the strip joints were (I am told) still at work. They rarely clothe and they never close.

12. THE INELUCTABLE MODALITY OF EXISTENCE

Mr A. Tim exhibits that paranoia for which his tribe is famous. He propounds a scenario in which Rangers and Celtic end the season joint top of the premier league with the same number of points, same number of games won, lost or drawn, and same number of goals for and against.

All things being equal, the Scottish League decides that the title will be decided by alphabetical order. A league official announces: 'The winners are Rangers FC and runners-up are The Celtic Football and Athletic Club.'

A chap who signs himself Moses Ramone e-mails with the suggestion: 'A law should be passed in the new Scottish parliament banning anyone committing to a football team before the age of 18. What other decision in life do you make so early that you have to remain with forever? Just ask me. At the age of 10, I made a very poorly informed decision based on too few facts.

'Society determines that maturity and age allows you to choose a political allegiance, a sexuality, and a wife – all of which you can change if the notion takes you. And does

anyone take the blindest bit of notice? But just try changing your footie team in late adult life.' Mr Ramone, a Glaswegian currently resident in London, is a St Mirren supporter.

Charlie Nicholas, the striker without equal of his day, has went on to become a pundit *sans pareil*. Commenting on an injury sustained by Paul Gascoigne, Charlie said: 'I think Paul has agitated his muscle.'

The literary style of *Trainspotting*, the seminal work by Irvine Welsh, was adopted and adapted by football fans of various persuasions. Like this piece, entitled 'Hunspotting':

Choose Rangers.
Choose all those failed attempts at the European Cup.
Choose to be knocked out of Europe ten times in nine seasons.
Choose a sectarian singing policy and then claim it never happens.
Choose funny handshakes.
Choose to walk down the middle of the road and not on the pavement.
Choose not to be liked by anyone and pretend not to care.

Choose to be the second team to win nine-in-a-row.
Choose 'Rule Britannia'.
Choose getting knocked out of three competitions by October.
Choose embarrassment.
Choose Rangers.

Then there was 'Timspotting':
Choose Celtic.
Choose bigotry.
Choose bending the knee towards Rome.
Choose the biscuit tin.
Choose paranoia.
Choose to let all your best players leave because of penny-pinching.
Choose living in the '60s.
Choose not being able to bring out a video for nine years.
Choose Mo Johnston but he didn't want to come.
Choose a bunnet.
Choose second best.
Choose Celtic.

And then there was 'Jagspotting':
Choose Partick Thistle.
Choose your local team.
Choose to ignore peer pressure in the playground.
Choose gay abandon and eternal optimism.
Choose to be non-sectarian.
Choose worthy self-righteousness.

shite COUNCIL

Choose the smartest strip in the league.
Choose to bask in former glory.
Choose to recite the 1971 team in the kitchen at parties.
Choose indulgent half-smiles from new business contacts.
Choose to want to punch Billy Connolly for his hurtful jibes.
Choose Chic Charnley.
Choose Heisenberg's uncertainty principle.
Choose Jaconelli's fish suppers.
Choose the ineluctable modality of existence.
Choose life.
Choose laughter.
Choose Partick Thistle.

A comment on the number of foreign players in the Scottish football leagues: 'I'm told of an incident at a recent match. A high ball came across. The goalkeeper ran out and shouted "Mine!" Two Bosnians and a Croatian ran off the pitch and up the tunnel.'

Some euphemisms used to describe less-than-talented footballers.

Schemer: can pass ball further than five yards to a member of his own team.

Provides width: too wee and frail to kick players in the midfield.

Long-serving: should have been sold years ago.

Stalwart: same as long-serving but dirty.

Jinking run: nearly fell over three times.

Rome has been added to the list of cities whence Scottish rugby folk must go to in support of their team. Whitecraigs Rugby Club and Murrayfield Wanderers, for example, produced a guide for their members' first trip to the Eternal City. It explains: 'The local currency is the Italian lira. There are hundreds of thousands of them to the pound (correct at time of going to press).'

And under places of interest it lists:

The Colosseum. Round building, mostly falling down, with lion droppings and dried blood on the floor.
Vatican City. Not really a city at all, since it has no McDonald's or red-light district.
The Spanish Steps. Really not very Spanish-looking at all.
Sistine Chapel. Don't know where it is, but worth looking out for.
Leaning Tower of Pisa. Very interesting but, alas, nowhere near Rome.

Their list of useful phrases for a quiet weekend in Rome includes:

Vorrei un avacatto che parli inglese – I would like a lawyer who speaks English.
Ho perso il portafoglio – I've lost my wallet.
Ho avuto gia in passato un attako cardiaco – I have had a heart attack.
Hai un bei sorriso – You have such a sweet smile (presumably only for use when being nice to Italian police officers at the match).

13. HONEY, WALT SHRUNK THE WORLD

APRIL 1998

America is the country which said bring me your poor, oppressed, huddled masses. But America was not all that keen to open its doors to this reporter when he turned up for a look at Disney's new Animal Kingdom theme park.

I had filled in the immigration entry form, stating that I was not visiting the US for purposes of international terrorism, genocide, drug trafficking, or moral turpitude. But this was not good enough. To enter the US for the purposes of scribbling a few words about Disney's latest tourist attraction required a certain kind of visa, which this accident-prone correspondent did not have.

The man in the immigration desk at Atlanta Airport seemed to take inordinate pleasure in listing the options open to him, the first being to send me back on the first available plane. Another option, which he magnanimously chose, was to offer a one-off, once in a lifetime, visa waiver for a fee of $95 in cash. They are a prickly and officious bunch, the US Immigration, and there are many things you should not say or even think while they are questioning you. Like

thinking that it was only Third World countries you had to pay a bribe to get in to. Or that you would have been quicker going to Mexico and swimming into the US across the Rio Grande. Or that it was easier to get into Cuba.

I waited until the visa was stamped, signed and issued before whistling a snatch of that tune about America being the land of the free. The irony, I fear, went right over the immigration officer's head.

The encounter meant that my connection to Orlando was long gone. With everyone and their auntie heading to Florida, the man at the Delta Airlines inconvenienced passenger desk could not say for sure when I would get a connection. After trying and failing to get me on three successive flights, he remarked that I was taking this bad news very well. I told him the reason for my cheery grin was that I had just phoned home to Scotland to hear that Aberdeen had beaten Glasgow Rangers 1–0 and that, furthermore, Amoruso had been sent off. The Delta man nodded nervously. This conversation may well have been a factor in his decision to get me out of there on the next flight to Orlando on another airline.

Air Trans is a small company operating out of Atlanta. It appears their speciality is whimsy. During the safety spiel before take-off, the attendant told us to put on our own oxygen masks first before helping children or, indeed, 'anyone at all childish' with theirs.

'Welcome to Cancun,' he said, joshingly, as we touched down at Orlando. Instead of asking passengers to remain seated, he told us: 'Keep your toosh on the cush till the safety belt sign is off.'

It was to be a suitable scene-setter for Orlando and the world of Disney. The Animal Kingdom is the fourth and largest theme park in Disney World. At 500 acres, it makes the Original Magic Kingdom appear a minor affair.

Disney boss Michael Eisner says that the Animal Kingdom is an appropriate venture for a company whose fortunes were initially based on two mice (Mickey and Minnie), two dogs (Goofy and Pluto), and a duck (Donald). The Animal Kingdom has 1,000 real, live animals, representing 200 species.

However, the predominant species is *Grossus Americanus*. The Fat Americans thrive in a habitat of fast food outlets. They can be seen all over Walt Disney World, waddling around with trays of food and drink. Constant grazing gives the Fat American that instantly recognisable rotund shape. Inside every thin American there is a Fat

American ready to break out. A phrase you're unlikely to hear in an American fast food court is: 'Try as I might, I just seem to be unable to put on weight.' It is not just the quantity of fodder consumed, but its fatty nature that has shaped the Fat American. Especially french fries. These were described for those not familiar with the dish in the Delta Airline magazine's 'Culinary America' section as 'potatoes sliced into long strips and deep fried in oil until golden brown. Considered a side dish, french fries are often enjoyed with ketchup or vinegar'.

Meanwhile, on to Disney World. A seasoned visitor advises me that the only way to deal with the whole experience is to check in my cynicism at the front desk. Having duly done so, I can admire the work of the imagineer. 'Imagineer' is the Disney word for the architects and designers who come up with the many and varied concepts within their theme parks. Undoubtedly the best question asked by the media on Animal Kingdom opening day was that by an Orlando radio journalist to a Disney employee: 'Did you ever imagine you'd become an imagineer?'

'No,' replied the imagineer.

Now that the imagineers have done their work, crack teams of Disney synergists, logisticians, statisticians, and publicists are bringing Animal Kingdom to the world's attention. Among the Animal Kingdom statistics: 4 million trees, shrubs, grasses, bushes, and vines were planted; 4.4 million cubic yards of soil was trucked in; 1,000 animals eat three tonnes of food a day (there are no figures for daily consumption by humans); the Animal Kingdom team travelled 500,000 miles during their research, a distance equal to circling the globe 20 times.

And another statistic: for the opening party, Disney laid on a week-long all-expenses paid trip for 3,000 journalists and provided lavish hospitality with endless quantities of food and drink. If these 3,000 journalists were laid end to end, no-one would be in the least surprised.

But back to the Animal Kingdom, where we can see the results of the imagineers' research. The Africa section centres on Harambe, a meticulous reconstruction of a Kenyan coastal town. The buildings are so authentically run-down and distressed you can almost believe that the Civil War is just over and the guerrilla forces, having inflicted the damage, have been driven out of town. It is only on

closer inspection that we see the dilapidated store is selling Disney accessories and the seedy hotel is actually the Tusker Rotisserie and Grill.

In Harambe, we constantly hear the authentic greeting 'Jambo'. Not a reference to Heart of Midlothian Football Club, but the Swahili for 'have a nice day'. The word 'Harambe' means 'with fries'. No, actually I imagineered that bit. Harambe means 'meeting place'.

Equally meticulous are the details of the jungle and savannah lands which comprise the 110-acre Kilimanjaro Safari Trail. Millions of dollars and much imagineering went into ensuring the roads are rutted to perfection, giving a genuine bumpy ride in the safari buses for the visitors.

With typical Disney efficiency, the animals were all in view. None of the 'You can't see it but there is a lion behind that rock 200 yards away' stuff of your average safari park.

Being a Disney attraction, it is not enough just to look at the lions, elephants, and giraffes on the Kilimanjaro Safari. There is a storyline about poachers in the game reserve, and each lorryload of visitors is called upon to go in hot pursuit and thwart these evil traders in ivory.

After the motorised safari, visitors are invited to indulge in the most un-American activity of walking. They stroll along the Gorilla Falls Trail, which takes in clearings where the aforementioned gorillas and other species can be viewed from behind plateglass partitions.

Faced with a constant procession of Fat Americans and progeny, the gorillas looked remarkably unfazed. The meercats – shy, timid, and normally ever-watchful – simply turned their backs. The hippos, in a hugely magnified version of a goldfish bowl, slumbered on and kept thinking it was Tuesday.

Another behind-the-glass experience was to be had at the Animal Kingdom Conservation Centre. There, Rolf Harris's *Animal Hospital*-style, visitors can watch vets carry out routine maintenance on the Kingdom's inmates. It tends to be nothing spectacular. When I was passing through, a vet was introducing a probe up a small lizard's backside. Something to do with salmonella, apparently.

Predictably, this new Disney venture has the animal rights movement mobilised against it. Equally predictable is that Disney has wheeled out a host of experts on wildlife conservation to

support their case. The UK journalists were treated to a wee talk by David Bellamy. Hired to give an 'independent' viewpoint, Bellamy admitted to being 'a Disney freak' and launched into something of a panegyric. We would come out of Animal Kingdom changed people, he said. The success of Animal Kingdom might close down the world's bad zoos. Animal Kingdom was nothing less than a gigantic Noah's ark. It would raise awareness of (and funds for) wildlife conservation.

There are obviously many animal rights issues to be investigated and discussed here. But I confess the question uppermost in my mind as I sat in the open-sided safari bus was how, in the absence of high fences and white hunters with guns, the beasts were to be kept under control. How would the Disney imagineers stop the lions getting at the gazelles, the cheetahs getting at the zebras, and, most importantly, any of them getting at me? 'The animals are separated in secret ways,' said a Disney publicist. 'We use naturalistic barriers,' said John Shields (no relation), chief imagineer of the safari ride.

Simba, the proud lion seen in majestic profile on the rocky outcrop a matter of 30 yards from the trail, would have to leap a mighty and unseen ravine to feast on a Fat American.

Of course, there will be accidents and the victims are more than likely to be the animals. US Federal investigators have cleared Disney of culpability in the deaths, so far, of 12 animals, including two exotic African birds run over by safari vehicles.

Mr Eisner, the Disney chief executive, may not have helped the Animal Kingdom image by a remark made during a live TV interview. Constantly interrupted by a squawking parrot in the background, he looked at the bird and said: 'Lunch? Parrot with fries.'

The conservation issue was summed up for me by the sign on a glass case at an Animal Kingdom interpretation centre. The inhabitant of the case was an Indigo snake, formerly a common species in the Orlando area but becoming increasingly rare 'because of urban development'. Presumably developments such as Animal Kingdom.

Irony abounds, not least the faithful recreation of a run-down Africa. What might be achieved if the money, effort, and ingenuity invested in Animal Kingdom had been diverted to a small country in Africa?

But that is fanciful romanticism. Disney's Africa is the real world of dollars-and-cents tourism. A world where a burger joint and shopping mall can be called the Rain Forest Cafe and it's not a joke.

It's a world where Disney has stolen the environmentalists' clothes by putting anti-logging graffiti on walls along the railway line. This message will be reinforced by a thrill ride still being built in the Asia section of Animal Kingdom. On the Tiger Rapids Run, visitors on a very safe and secure raft take a twist in the river to find the jasmine-scented jungle has turned into 'a denuded slope of logged-out forests burning out of control'.

Disney are hot on environmental stuff like recycling. And they ask their visitors to make sacrifices. The Pizzafari fast food facility in Animal Kingdom has a sign saying: 'In the spirit of environmentality and to protect our animals from harm we do not offer straws and lids.' Meanwhile, over in Dinoland in the Restaurantosaurus, customers are tucking into meals that would keep an African village going for a week. The food comes in 'dinosaur portions', and in the land of the Fat American that is a fair chunk of the world's resources.

There are heavy educational overtones to Animal Kingdom. I'm not sure how this will go down with the average tourist who has paid $44 to get in. Frankly, the imagineers have gone a bit worthy on us. The centrepiece of the park is the Tree of Life, a 145ft-high concrete structure built around a redundant oil platform. You would expect Disney to use this for a rollercoaster or similar thrill ride. Instead, it has been turned into a giant semi-figurative sculpture with 103,000 (sorry, that statistic just slipped out there) transparent green leaves that actually blow in the wind. There is fun to be had, obviously. Inside the Tree of Life is a 430-seat auditorium which houses *It's Tough to be a Bug*, an absolutely brilliant 3D show about insects. It is an assault on all the senses and, thankfully, the insect characters involved have been Disneyfied. If real images had been used the audience would be reduced to quivering wrecks.

Away from the relative vagaries of genuine wildlife, Animal Kingdom is on a sounder and more familiar footing with what Disney call their 'Humanimals'. These are people in animal costumes. Or cast members, as they are called. Everyone at Disney World is a cast member, from the dustman to the man in the Goofy suit. All the favourite characters from *The Jungle Book*, *The Lion King* and *Pocahontas* are there. But there was no sign of Bambi, not even on a menu.

 TOM SHIELDS GOES FORTH

With fine attention to detail, these humanimal spectaculars take place in auditoriums which smell of wildlife. The imagineers call it 'odorisation'.

Animal Kingdom was a decade in the making and cost a couple of billion dollars. As a first-time visitor to Walt Disney World, I have to say it does not top my list of attractions. It lacks the charm of the Magic Kingdom, the pizzazz of Disney MGM Studios and the good food of the Epcot Centre. Highlights of Disney World for me were the *Pirates of the Caribbean* show in the Magic Kingdom. You sail around a harbour town while animated figures enact scenes of unspeakable debauchery, senseless violence, and wanton cruelty. Just like Millport on September Weekend.

At Epcot, there is much fun as you become insect-sized in *Honey I Shrank the Audience*. At Disney MGM the best bit is the Tower of Terror, where you plunge 13 floors in a lift in a derelict haunted hotel.

There are occasional down moments in Disney, like when you attend a 'Character Breakfast' and sundry people in furry suits come in to greet you. I would like at this point to apologise for telling Goofy to 'feck off'. He or she was only doing his or her job, cuddling me and patting me on the head. In mitigation I would say that Disney had put on a really good party the night before and the effects were still with me. Pluto by comparison was a bit of a bad dog, rubbing himself against the chair of the young woman at the breakfast table. He was obviously in heat. Mickey, of course, was the perfect gentleman.

There were surreal moments, too. One of the fairground attractions at the Downtown Disney entertainment complex is called Flippin' the Chicken. You put a plastic chicken on to a metal launch pad device which, when hit by a hammer, sends the chicken flying in the general direction of a rotating circular stove. The idea is to land the chicken in one of the pots on the stove. The Flippin' the Chicken stall was being run by a girl from Guatemala. The girl, presumably an economic refugee from Central America, looked bored and possibly slightly bewildered by the proceedings.

In between failing to flip chickens into pots, I wondered if the girl had ever written home to her family to say she was now a Disney cast member and had a good job supervising gringos trying to flip plastic chickens into pots on top of a fake stove. She would

presumably enclose some of her hard-earned dollars, so that her family could buy a real chicken or two.

Regardless of this writer's reservations about Animal Kingdom, the visitors will turn up in their millions. Disney World will continue to expand. It is an autonomous state, covering 43 square miles and employing 50,000 people. The swamp and scrubland of central Florida has been turned into the world's playground, with 50 million visitors a year, 1.2 million of them British.

The theme parks, hotel resorts and entertainment complexes are the physical embodiment of the colonisation of the world by Disney's films and videos. It reaches all parts of society. Even the American military have their own private corner of Disney World.

In days gone by, only the rich could afford to travel to foreign parts. Common folk were diverted when the circus came to town. Now the circus is Disney World, and mass transit means the world can come to the circus.

They come to Animal Kingdom to see Africa and Asia. They come to Epcot to see Disney's pasteurised and homogenised versions of 11 countries, from Morocco to Mexico.

In more ways than one, Honey, Walt Shrank The World.

14. THE MULL POLICE DISMITHESS US

We were sent this basis for biblical or theological debate.

THREE PROOFS THAT JESUS WAS JEWISH:

He went into his father's business
He lived at home until he was 33
He was sure his mother was a virgin, and his mother was sure he was
   God

THREE PROOFS THAT JESUS WAS IRISH:

He never got married
He was always telling stories
He loved green pastures

THREE PROOFS THAT JESUS WAS PUERTO RICAN:

His first name was Jesus
He was bilingual
He was always being harassed by the authorities

THREE PROOFS THAT JESUS WAS ITALIAN:

He talked with his hands
He had wine with every meal
He set up his HQ in Rome

THREE PROOFS THAT JESUS WAS BLACK:

He called everybody 'brother'
He liked Gospel
He couldn't get a fair trial

THREE PROOFS THAT JESUS WAS A HIPPY:

He never cut his hair
He walked around barefoot
He started a new religion

THREE PROOFS THAT JESUS WAS A WOMAN:

He had to feed a crowd, at a moment's notice, from a few leftovers
He kept trying to get the message across to a bunch of men who just
    didn't get it
Even when he was dead, he had to get up because there was more
    work to do.

TALES OF THE MULL POLIS

We hear of an officer who, concerned that the force could not provide him with a shredder machine, used his initiative. He started using his bairn's two hamsters to dispose of unwanted documents.

An officer based on the island telephones Strathclyde Police's forensic department in Glasgow and says: 'If I send you down some of yon skelp, can you test it for me?' The forensic scientist asks for further details of the item to be analysed and is told: 'It's yon broon powder the weans use.'

'Don't you mean smack?' asks the forensic person.

'Aye, that'll be right,' says our rural bobby. 'Ah kent it was something to dae wi' hittin' folk.'

Our tales about the police on Mull led to us being taken to task on the subtle cadences of the local language. The following are examples of correct Mullese.

An irate grocer on Mull told his message boy: 'You're here an' you're no' away yet. The next time I am sending a fool I will go myself.'

And conversation with a local roadman:
'Hey, Lachie, what's taking you home so early?'
Says Lachie: 'I'm going home to change my wet clothes.'
'But it's no' rainin' yet.'
To which Lachie replies: 'Ach, yes, but it will be before I get home.'

Advertisement for Fairy Liquid which never got made: 'Mummy, why are your hands so soft?'

The mother replies: 'Because I'm only 12.'

We are told, but alas have no way of checking, that the following are actual replies sent to the Child Support Agency, following inquiries about the identity of the fathers:

I don't know the identity of the father of my daughter. He drives a BMW that now has a hole made by my stiletto in one of the door panels. Perhaps you can contact BMW service stations in this area and see if he's had it replaced.

I cannot tell you the name of child A's Dad as he informs me that to do so would blow his cover and that would have cataclysmic implications for the British economy. I am torn between doing right by you and right by my country. Please advise.

From the dates it seems that my daughter was conceived at Euro Disney. Maybe it really is the Magic Kingdom.

So much about that night is a blur. The only thing that I remember for sure is Delia Smith did a programme about eggs earlier in the evening. If I'd stayed in and watched TV rather than going to a party, mine might have remained unfertilised.

I am unsure as to the identity of the father of my child as I was being sick out of a window when taken unexpectedly from behind. I can provide you with a list of names of men I think were at the party.

The scene is an identification parade at a Glasgow police station. The six young men, including the suspect, are asked in turn to speak the words: 'Just give me the money and shut up.'

They do so with the exception of one (guess who?), who blurts out: 'On the advice of my solicitor, I have nothing to say.'

An American tourist desperate to see as much of Scotland as possible asks the owners of a bed and breakfast establishment at Kilmartin where he can catch a ferry to go to Tenenay.

Baffled by a name they have never heard of, a map is consulted until they realise the poor chap is referring to Iona.

Some kilted followers of the Scotland team have a habit, when inebriated, of hoisting said garment to reveal its contents. 'What do you think of that then, hen?' asked one fan in London.

Her reply was: 'Not a lot.'

More subtle ripostes:
    So that's why you're supposed to judge people on personality.
    Can I be honest with you? This explains your car.
    It's OK. We'll work round it.
    Oh look, just like a willie – but smaller.
    No thanks, I roll my own.

Into the already complicated world that is Northern Ireland has been thrust the issue of the Ulster-Scots langauage. This nebulous (as some call it) language is being brought into official government use. Northern Ireland Health and Social Services advertised for an Equality Schemes Manager. This post came out in Scots-Irish, according to the advert, as an Eeksi-Peeksi Skame Heid-Yin. The salary, though, is not be laughed at, coming in at over £32,000 with, presumably, quite a rush for the application form to be 'fult in'.

Another post to be filled was that of sub-editor for Hansard, or the Chaummer o tha Scrievit Accoont, as it will also be known. The Assembly wants a sub-editor with: 'A perfit guid hannlin o tha Inglis, takin in gin yer fit or no fur tae owreset the wurds spake intil aisy read scrievin, houlin tha much ye can o tha taakeris ain wyes an gates.'

This, as you can instantly tell, means they are looking for someone with a thorough command of English, including the ability to turn the spoken word into easily readable narrative, retaining as much as possible of the speaker's style and idiom.

As usual, the advert states there will be no discrimination, irrespective of age, race, religion, gender, or political opinion. We like that last one, which is translated as 'quhit pairtie ye houl wi'. Maybe there is more to this language than we realise.

**Welcome to
EMBO
Twinned with
KAUNAKAKAI
HAWAII
Please drive
carefully**

Some of the first manifestations of the bilingual approach are street signs in both English and Ulster Scots. This did not go down too well in the loyalist Clonduff estate, where Castlereagh council had unveiled signs which read 'Tullyard Way' in English and 'Heichbrae Eirt' in Ulster Scots. It was almost immediately pulled down by loyalists who assumed the second wording was Irish.

In County Armagh, there is a place called Drumnahunsion. As part of the move to include Irish on signs, there was a suggestion that 'Droim na h'Uinseann' be added. If you look closely at both versions, you might agree that the English and the Irish are remarkably similar. But not from the point of view of one angry resident, who fumed: 'Over my dead body will they give Drumnahunsion a Gaelic name.'

Meanwhile, we hear of a Unionist councillor who complained about 'no smoking' signs in Irish on Belfast buses. The foreign language was, in fact, French.

Bill Speirs, general secretary of the STUC, was delighted to be presented with an honorary doctorship from Paisley University. But then he was harangued by his colleagues with a string of doctor jokes to torment him in case he ever tries to use the title Dr Speirs.

Among the best/worst that they flung at him included: 'Doctor, doctor, I can't say the letters f, n, or t.'

'Well, you can't say fairer than that then.'

And then there is the old joke-book classic: 'Doctor, why do you have a thermometer behind your ear?'

'Because some bum has my pencil.'

The revocation of the Act of Settlement which would allow members of the royal family to marry Catholics was discussed in Glasgow's City Chambers. This prompted one of those present to ask: 'Does this mean that there is now a chance we'll get a Protestant as Lord Provost?'

We hear of a visit paid by the New Zealand Prime Minister, Mrs Shipley, to an Elderly Persons' Place of Residence. On entering a room she asked one resident: 'Do you know who I am?'

'No,' was the reply, 'but if you go to the front desk they'll tell you.'

Our politicians tied themselves in knots over the debate on Section 28. We pass on without comment the reaction of Clydesdale MP Jimmy Hood, who says: 'I personally find it very difficult to be whipped through the Government lobby without copper bottom guarantees that the promotion of homosexuality in our classrooms will be prohibited.'

We hear of an informed debate in a Paisley pub between a teacher and a parent on the merits and demerits of removing Section 28, the law limiting discussion of homosexuality in Scottish schools. The teacher can see arguments for and against. The parent offers an unusual slant on the topic. He is keen to keep Section 28 as, he explains, 'It prevents history teachers telling the kids that King Billy was a poof.'

15. MIXED DOUBLES

One of the daily tasks of the Diary is to provide those readers who have finished the *Herald* crossword with exercise for the grey matter. Alison Campbell of Portobello came up with the simple and entertaining concept of bringing together great historical couples.

Alison set the ball rolling with Harry and Estée Lauder; Charles and Jackie Kennedy; Gordon and Divine Brown; Bonnie and Crocodile Dundee; and Jock and Gertrude Stein. Readers responded with:

Homer and Wallis Simpson
Charles and Barbara Windsor
Benjamin and Aretha Franklin
Willie and Diana Ross
El and Juliet Greco
Damon and Fanny Hill
Patrick and Demi Moore
Helen and St Mirren
PC and Iris Murdoch
Craig and Daphne Broon
Gie's A and Goldie Hawn
Wat and Bonnie Tyler
Capability and Charlie Brown
    (they will design your garden
    for peanuts)
Augustus and Bible John
Ghengis and Fergus McKhan
Henry and Anna Ford (any
    news, so long as it's black)
Debbie and Dirty Harry (do
    you feel lucky, hen?)
Calvin and Rita Coolidge
Farley and Rita Rusk

Sara and Robert E. Lee – icing on the wedding cake
Ron and Dickie Davies
Hugh and *Debbie Does Dallas*
Pope John and Dorothy Paul

Remy and Millicent Martin
The Desert and Samantha Fox
Cary and Student Grant – both deceased

If Isla St Clair married Barry White, would she become Isla White? And if she then divorced Barry and married Bryan Ferry, would she be Isla White Ferry?

If Nick Faldo's caddie Fanny Sunesson married Vijay Singh, would that make her Fanny Singh?

What about Carrie Fisher, actor in Star Wars, marrying Phil Oakey, lead singer of the Human League, and becoming Carrie Oakey?

If Stevie Nicks married William Shatner, would she become Stevie Shatner-Nicks?

If Liz Hurley married Craig Burley, would she become Liz Hurley-Burley?

If Geri Halliwell married James Caan, would she become a Geri Caan?

Into the indelicate area of the *ménage a trois*: if Una McLean, Paloma Picasso, and Serge Blanco all got together we could have Una Paloma Blanco. (Yes, we know it should be paloma blanca.)

On the subject of names which merge to make something totally different, might a future James Bond movie combine the characters Blofeld and Oddjob?

16. A WEE CHAT WITH THE HEAD OF NATO

APRIL 2000

Lord Robertson of Port Ellen is arguably the most powerful Scotsman in the world. George Robertson (as was) plies his new trade as Secretary-General of Nato from a remarkably unremarkable office in a complex in Brussels which has much in common with Cumbernauld early-1960s architecture.

The Diary first came across Mr Robertson in 1978. The battle terrain then for the young whisky industry union official was the Hamilton by-election. The opponent was Margo MacDonald. He won, of course, and embarked upon a political career which now sees him at the head of a military alliance of 19 nations.

Having been allocated a generous 45 minutes from the Secretary-General's schedule, I was able to ask him such questions as: 'Did your time working for the General Municipal and Boilermakers Union prepare you for running Nato?'

Lord Robertson said: 'I thought this was supposed to be serious, Shields.'

He had a point. His is a very serious job. A brief overheard

conversation between Lord Robertson with Jamie Shea, his media adviser, took in topics such as French soldiers hurt that day in Kosovo, a spot of bother in Montenegro, and something about talks with the Russians about closer contacts.

Fortunately, George Robertson of Dunblane has retained his sense of humour, and related: 'People ask me how I feel about being transported in huge cavalcades and being constantly saluted. I reply that I had quite forgotten what it was like to be a GMB official.'

The negotiating skills picked up by the young Robertson of the GMB and honed in years of Labour politics are now being tested on a larger canvas. His big challenge is Nato's relations with Russia. 'At the time of the Kosovo conflict, the Russians said Nato was an aggressor intent on genocide,' says Robertson of the Cold War iciness which had come back into the military equation. 'But now we are talking again.'

Lord Robertson has done a lot of talking since he took up the Nato job last autumn. He has now visited all 19 countries involved in the alliance. His conversation is peppered with the names of prime ministers and presidents. But it is a meeting in the Ukraine with schoolchildren which is his abiding memory. They were 15-year-olds from the Magnet School No.155 in Kiev. A magnet school is a centre of excellence, a bit like George's own alma mater, Dunoon Grammar, which also produced Labour's John Smith and Brian Wilson, and the *Herald*'s own late and much-missed Robert McLaughlan.

You can trust bright school weans to get to the heart of the matter. 'What were you doing when you were 15 years old like us, and did you think then you would become Secretary-General of Nato?' one of them asked.

'I told them that at 15 I was protesting outside the US navy nuclear base in Dunoon and that also answered the second part of the question.' Lord Robertson can still quote great chunks of the CND song book from those halcyon days, including such phrases as 'We dinnae want Polaris'. In an unusual step for a CND supporter, he has addressed the nuclear issue by becoming one of the people in charge of the dread arsenal.

One of the Kiev schoolgirls asked Lord Robertson: 'When was the first time you fell in love?' He referred to his 30-year marriage to Sandra, and said diplomatically that he would rather talk about the last time he fell in love.

A memento of the Ukraine visit sits on the mantelpiece in his office. It is a bottle of vodka in the shape of a rifle. The gift, from the Ukrainian military, has a label bearing the Union Jack and a photo of Lord Robertson. It sits beside his collection of malt whiskies from his native island of Islay. The bottles remain unopened. Lord Robertson obviously does not drink on duty.

 TOM SHIELDS GOES FORTH 145

GOLF BALL SHAGGER

- PICKS UP PRACTICE BALLS WITH NO BENDING OVER

- EQUIPED WITH A HEAVY-DUTY ANODIZED ALUMINUM TUBE WITH AUTOMATIC DIRT RELEASE DESIGN FOR NO BUILD-UP

- DURABLE NYLON BAG HOLDS UP TO 75 GOLF BALLS

- COLLAPSES FOR EASY TRANSPORTATION AND STORAGE

- ZIPPERED BAG FOR EASY REMOVAL

Also on the mantelpiece is a photograph of the Robertson family house in Port Ellen. 'The cottage is only about 20ft from the North Atlantic, quite appropriate for someone who was to work for the North Atlantic Treaty Organisation,' Lord Robertson says. He adds: 'My Scottishness does not go unnoticed.' When he met Vladimir Putin, the Russian leader mentioned that he had been to Edinburgh. Robertson wanted to find out more detail, but never did, because other, rather more important topics of arms limitation and Chechenya intruded.

When he was in Poland for a meeting with President Aleksander Krasniewski, who should Lord Robertson encounter but Jan Stepek, the Polish Lanarkshire business entrepreneur and former chairman of Hamilton Accies football club. Though no longer bound to Hamilton by constituency duties, Robertson retains an affection for the local football team and is concerned about its current refugee status. 'I can see ways of stopping the world blowing itself up. I can see ways to repair the wounds between nations,' he says. 'But I don't see how to solve the problems of the Accies.'

So, would Lord Robertson rather be back in Scotland participating in the new politics of his own nation? The answer is no. For one thing, in his old capacity as Shadow Scottish Secretary, he has bitter memories of being mauled by the media and others over the detail of the devolution referendum. But his work bore fruit in the shape of the Scots Parliament. He is still waiting for the thanks of a grateful nation.

While old comrades agonise on the Mound, Lord Robertson goes state-hopping.

One day's work included breakfast in Oslo, lunch in Copenhagen, and dinner in Iceland. He is a particular fan of David Oddsson, the Icelandic prime minister. 'They swapped joke for joke,' chips in spin doctor Dr Shea, from an adjacent sofa where he is monitoring the Secretary-General of Nato's interview with Pepys the Elder. The Icelandic premier, greeting Shimon Peres of Israel on a recent visit to Iceland, said: 'You are the chosen people, we are the frozen people.'

Robertson's own canon of humour includes the story of a Belgrade resident who is charged nine dinars for a litre of milk. The shopkeeper explains why it is so expensive: three dinars for the milk, three dinars to pay for the reconstruction of the city, and three dinars towards building Slobodan Milosevic's son's new disco. He

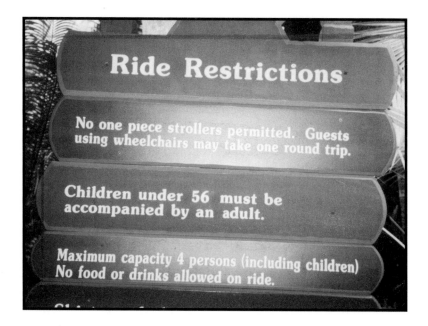

Ride Restrictions

No one piece strollers permitted. Guests using wheelchairs may take one round trip.

Children under 56 must be accompanied by an adult.

Maximum capacity 4 persons (including children) No food or drinks allowed on ride.

returns the next day and is told the price is six dinars. Why the reduction, he asks. Today we have no milk, the shopkeeper replies.

When Lord Robertson flies about on Nato business, he has 19 air forces at his disposal. On his recent trip to Moscow, he flew Luftwaffe. When he returns to Scotland, as he does frequently, he goes by scheduled airline while his subordinate, the Supreme Allied Commander of Nato, has his own plane. When he is being George Robertson back in Dunblane, he is, of course, discreetly but substantially guarded. His security men will have seen the interior of the odd Scottish pub. One or two have been exposed to the delights of Dunoon on a wet Sunday when the Secretary-General visits his father.

I asked Lord Robertson what he is nowadays. A military man at the head of an estimated 4.5 million troops? A politician still? The latter, says Lord Robertson. But in conversation with Putin, George mentioned that he comes from four generations of policemen. Putin said this made him a 'super policeman'. George Robertson, the world's Supercop.

17. THE WHEELBARROW POSITION

Noël Coward's witty and sophisticated play *Cavalcade* played at the Citizens Theatre to an appreciative audience, but staff were surprised when three nuns with 15 children in tow arrived to watch it. Discreet inquiries discovered they thought they had booked for a resurrection of that old Scottish Television show, *Glen Michael's Cavalcade*.

We are told of one Western Isles couple who decided to liven up their sex life by ordering the manual *The Joy of Sex*. After a lengthy perusal, Lachlan said to his wife, Morag: 'Would you like to try the wheelbarrow position?'

'What's that?' she asked.

'Well, I grab you by the legs like we used to during those wheelbarrow races when we were at school.'

Morag thinks about it, and tells him: 'Well, OK – just as long as we don't go past my mother's.'

li Abassi of Radio Scotland gets away with being non-PC. 'Do you know why black soldiers have the highest casualty rate in the British Army?' he asks. 'It's because when they're on the battlefield and the officer shouts "Get down!" they all stand up and dance.'

story from the Christmas party season involving staff from a Glasgow hospital on their night out. After much drink had been taken, a couple who had just met that night went back to the woman's house for a night of torrid hanky-panky.

Afterwards, the man said: 'You're a surgeon, aren't you?'

When she asked how he knew, he pointed out that she spent 15 minutes in the bathroom scrupulously scrubbing up before going to bed. 'And I bet you're an anaesthetist,' she replied.

'Now how did you know that?' he asked.

'Because I didn't feel a thing,' she told him.

oman to eager but unwelcome suitor: 'I'm not your type. I'm not inflatable.'

ept of We Think We Know What They Mean. The *Ayr Advertiser* reports that local consultant Dr Leo Murray is off to the Isle of Skye: 'He will be joining a team of two other doctors, who will replace the island's retiring single-handed surgeon.'

he polis can have a nice way with words. We hear of a cop who described a colleague, something of a loose cannon, as 'an accident looking for a locus'.

18. CATS

INSTRUCTIONS ON GIVING YOUR CAT A PILL:

Pick up cat, and cradle as if holding a baby. Position forefinger and thumb on either side of cat's mouth and gently apply pressure to cheeks. As cat opens mouth, pop pill in. Allow cat to close mouth and swallow. Retrieve pill from floor, and cat from behind sofa. Repeat process.

Retrieve cat from bedroom, throw soggy pill away, take new pill from foil wrap. Cradle cat in left arm holding rear paws tightly with left hand. Force jaws open and push pill to back of mouth with right forefinger. Hold mouth shut for a count of ten.

Retrieve pill from goldfish bowl and cat from top of wardrobe. Call spouse from garden. Kneel on floor with cat wedged firmly between knees, hold front and rear paws. Get spouse to hold head firmly with one hand while forcing wooden ruler into mouth. Drop pill down ruler and rub cat's throat vigorously.

Retrieve cat from curtain rail, get another pill from foil wrap. Make note to repair curtains. Sweep shattered Doulton figures from hearth. Wrap cat in large towel with head just visible. Get spouse to hold cat and towel firmly under armpit. Put pill in end

of drinking straw, force mouth open with pencil, and blow down drinking straw.

Check to make sure pill not harmful to humans, drink glass of water to take taste away. Apply bandage to spouse's forearm and remove blood from carpet with cold water and soap.

Retrieve cat from neighbour's shed. Get another pill. Place cat in cupboard and close door on neck with head showing. Force mouth open with dessert spoon. Flick pill down throat with elastic band.

Put door back on hinges. Ring fire brigade to retrieve cat from tree across the road. Take last pill from foil wrap. Tie cat's front paws to rear paws with garden twine and bind tightly to leg of dining table. Find heavy duty pruning gloves in shed, force cat's mouth open with small spanner. Push pill into mouth followed by large piece of fillet steak and half-pint of water.

Get spouse to drive you to casualty. Sit quietly while doctor stitches fingers and forearm and removes pill remnants from right eye. Call at furniture shop on way home to order new table.

Go to vet, who puts cat on table. Cat lies there while vet pops open mouth and drops in pill. Cat swallows pill. Vet says: 'See how easy it is?'

A CAT'S GUIDE ON HOW TO TRAIN OWNERS:

Doors. Do not allow closed doors in any room. To get door opened, stand on hind legs and hammer with forepaws. Once door is opened, it is not necessary to use it. After you have managed to get an outside door opened, stand halfway in and out and think about several things. This is particularly important during very cold weather, rain, or snow.

If you have to throw up, get to a chair quickly. If you cannot manage in time, get to an Oriental rug. When throwing up on the carpet, make sure you move backwards simultaneously so that the result is as long as a human's bare foot.

Bathrooms. Always accompany guests to the bathroom. It is not necessary to do anything. Just sit and stare.

Helping/hampering. When supervising cooking, sit just behind the left heel of the cook. You cannot be seen, and thereby stand a better chance of being stepped on and then picked up and comforted. For book readers, get in close under the chin, between eyes and book, unless you can lie across the book itself. For knitting projects or paperwork, lie on the work so as to obscure as much as possible. Pretend to doze, but every so often reach out and slap the pencil or knitting needles. When dislodged, watch sadly from the side of the table. When activity is proceeding nicely, roll around on the papers. After being removed for the second time, push pens off the table, one at a time.

Newspapers. When a human is holding the newspaper in front of him or her, be sure to leap on it. They love to jump.

Walking. Dart quickly and as close as possible in front of the human, especially on stairs, when they have something in their arms, in the dark, and when they first get up in the morning. This will help their coordination skills.

Science and perpetual motion. One theory proposes: 'When a cat is dropped it always lands on its feet, and when toast is dropped, it always lands buttered side down. Therefore, if a slice of toast is strapped to a cat's back, buttered side up, and the animal is then dropped, the two opposing forces will cause it to hover, spinning inches above the ground. If enough toast-laden felines were used, they could form the basis of a high-speed monorail system.'

It is hard to understand, as one chap observed, why women love cats. As he explained: 'Cats are independent, they don't listen, they don't come in when you call, they like to stay out all night, come home when it suits them, and expect to be fed and stroked, then want to be left alone and sleep.

'So it seems that every quality that women hate in a man, they love in a cat.'

19. YOU'VE LEFT YOUR INJUN RUNNING

A sighting in deepest Drumchapel (a garden suburb of Glasgow) of an ice cream van with striking livery and unusual slogan. The van was bright pink with images of Mickey Mouse and various pals. The legend read: 'The Disney Half Taste Nice Van'.

A van in Glasgow's Milton was emblazoned with the politically incorrect message: 'For straight hair and curly teeth – eat mair sweeties!'

The death of Clayton Moore, star of the *Lone Ranger* TV cowboy serial, provoked a flood of childhood memories . . . and bad jokes.

The Lone Ranger and Tonto arrived at a hotel on a bitterly cold night, and when told there was no room for his companion, the Lone Ranger instructed Tonto to keep warm by jogging round the block until the problem was resolved.

Eventually the manager came in and said to the Lone Ranger: 'Can I help you? And by the way, do you know you've left your injun running?'

We're just sorry we raised the subject.

The Lone Ranger and Tonto are making their way to Dodge City on horseback when they get attacked by a mob of Sioux Indians. They both gallop away with the Indians hot on their heels, firing many arrows in their general direction. This goes on for a few miles until our heroes manage to get to the safety of Dodge City.

They get off their horses. Tonto is pulling arrows out of his back, his legs, and his arms. He looks at the Lone Ranger who is immaculate, without a scratch on him, and says: 'Kemo Sabe, how come I've been hit at least 20 times and you haven't been touched?'

The Lone Ranger replies: 'It's my new aftershave, Tonto. Aramis.'

The Lone Ranger comes across Tonto, prone on the trail with his ear pressed to the dirt. 'Stagecoach pass this way one hour ago, Kemo Sabe. Driver a big man with a black beard. Passenger carry shotgun and smoke cigar.'

'That's amazing, Tonto. How do you know?'

'Because it ran over my head.'

A wee fellow dauners into the chemist's shop and asks to talk to the pharmacist. Looking around furtively, he asks: 'Do you sell Viagra?'

The pharmacist answers in the affirmative.

The wee man says: 'Do you think I could get it over the counter?'

The pharmacist looks at him for a moment and says: 'Maybe, if you took six pills at once.'

E-mail is not the most romantic method of sending a Valentine. You think you've sent your loved one a simple message such as 'I Love You', and sit back happy and content at the impact it will have. What you have forgotten, of course, is that she will have scrolled to the bottom of the e-mail, where she will be told: 'The information contained in this message does not constitute an offer or an acceptance of an offer, nor shall it form any part of a legally binding contract.

'No representation is made as to its accuracy, and no liability can be accepted for any loss arising from the use of any of the information in it.

'It is not guaranteed to be free from any viruses and it is strongly recommended that you check for such viruses. If you are not the

intended recipient we would be grateful if you could permanently erase the message and any attachments from your equipment.

'E-mail is an informal method of communication and is subject to possible data corruption. For these reasons it will normally be inappropriate to rely upon information contained in an e-mail without obtaining tangible written confirmation of it.'

Adam McNaughton, an astute observer of Glasgow, from jeely pieces to Cathcart buses, has noticed the shopping centre culture which has become prevalent in the city. He has paraphrased Julius Caesar's famous saying into a Glasgow context. It now reads 'Veni, Vidi, Visa'. Which means: 'I came, I had a look around, I did a lot of shopping.'

The weans in a class of eight-year-olds have reassembled, bright-eyed and pony-tailed, after the Christmas holidays. The teacher, who had devoted many hours the previous term to the story of the Nativity, asked the pupils to write their own version of what occurred in Bethlehem. She was impressed to see that one of the normally less diligent boys was into the second folio of his essay. He spoiled it somewhat by putting up his hand and asking: 'Excuse me, miss. Whit wis it Mary had, a boy or a girl?'

A chap who has taken early retirement is failing to do all the little jobs around the house that his wife has timetabled for him. To keep her quiet, he agrees to have a check-up with the doctor about why he can't do as much work as he used to.

After a thorough examination, he says to the doctor: 'I can take it. Tell it to me straight, in plain English, what's wrong with me.' Having found nothing at all, the exasperated doctor tells him: 'In plain English, you're just a lazy old fart.'

'Thanks,' said the man. 'Now give me the medical term, so I can tell my wife.'

A chap tells his mates that he's sorry, but he can't make it to the pub that night as his wife is doing bird impersonations – she is watching him like a hawk.

Then there is the man who affectionately calls his wife Spiderwoman. 'She's always telling me I've got her climbing the walls.'

> **unattended children will be SOLD as slaves**

An insight into the real meaning of some of the terms used by women in lonely hearts adverts:

40ish – 48
Adventurer – has had more partners than you ever will
Beautiful – pathological liar
Emotionally secure – takes medication
Free spirit – smokes dope
Friendship first – trying to live down reputation as a slut
Fun – annoying
Open-minded – desperate
Professional – what a witch
Romantic – looks better by candle light
Wants soulmate – one step away from stalking

And what men really mean in their adverts:

40-ish – 52 and looking for 25-year-old
Athletic – sits on couch watching Sky Sports
Educated – feels he can treat you like an idiot
Good looking – arrogant
Honest – pathological liar
Likes to cuddle – insecure and overly dependent
Open-minded – wants to sleep with your sister as well

Physically fit – spends a lot of time in front of mirror admiring
  himself
Poet – once drunkenly scrawled a verse on a toilet wall
Stable – occasional stalker, but never arrested
  Thoughtful – says 'please' when he wants you to get him a beer

Tim goes into a confessional box and says: 'Bless me, Father, for I have sinned. I have been with a loose woman.'

The priest says: 'Is that you, Tim?'

'Yes, Father, it's me.'

'Who was the woman you were with?'

'I cannot tell you, Father, because I don't want to ruin her reputation.'

The priest asks: 'Was it Brenda O'Malley?'

'No, Father.'

'Was it Mary MacDonald?'

'No.'

'Was it Catriona MacLeod?'

'No.'

'Was it Mary Elizabeth O'Shea?'

'No, Father.'

'Was it Catherine Anne Geraghty?'

'No, Father.'

'Was it Cathy Morgan?'

'No, Father. I cannot tell you.'

The priest finally says: 'Tim, I admire your perseverance, but you must atone for your sins. Your penance will be four Our Fathers and five Hail Marys.'

Tim walks back to his pew and sits next to his pal, Sean, who slides over and whispers: 'What happened?'

Tim says: 'Well, I got four Our Fathers, five Hail Marys, and six good leads.'

A young Scotswoman was sent by an international company to the classy Waldorf Astoria Hotel in New York to help organise a Burns Supper for 200 of the company's executives. It was hard work ensuring everything was going to be ready, but just when she was sure she had thought of everything, the Waldorf's functions manager said to her: 'Just a suggestion. This Mr Burns you are organising the

birthday celebration for. Shouldn't we organise a cake for him?'

A correspondent of the Diary organised a Burns Supper for the various nationalities with whom she works at the Technical University of Denmark. But alas, the national bard is perhaps not as universally known as we would have hoped. We were told: 'Arrangements seemed to be going well and I told a German couple to spread the word among some mutual friends that the Burns Supper would happen this week sometime. Word spread somewhat rapidly, I discovered, when I bumped into another German in the canteen. "I hear you are having a Richard Burton evening," he said. "Sounds interesting."'

O verheard in Sauchiehall Street, two ladies in their prime discussing the wording on a recently purchased cosmetics container. 'This disnae sound too promising oan the shagging front. It says antirides.'

Antirides, the Diary's beauty consultant tells us, is French for anti-wrinkle.

L ondoners fed up with Americans boasting about how everything in their country is bigger, better, wider, and so on, have a new ploy. If they are showing an American the Millennium Wheel at the Thames, they can point it out, pause, then announce dramatically: 'And wait till you see the size of the hamster.'

E dinburgh waiting staff can be a bit sniffy at times. A chap from Sussex decided to return to Edinburgh where he had fond memories of his student days. Sitting in his favourite restaurant, he told the waiter: 'You know, it's been more than five years since I first came in here.'

'You'll have to wait your turn, sir,' replied the harassed waiter. 'I can only serve one table at a time.'

U nsuccessful chat-up lines. This example involves a Scottish chap based in London who meets a female compatriot. His patter is not working, so he plays the tartan card by saying how nice it is to meet a fellow Scot. 'What's your name?' he asks.

'It's Elaine. As in leave me,' she replies.

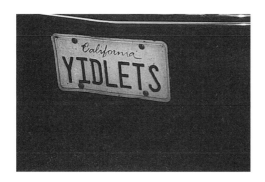

We desperately hope that the teacher was joking when she told us that, at a Renfrewshire nursery, the nursery nurse took out a set of weighing scales to show the three-year-olds. Asking if anybody knew what it was, a little boy piped up: 'Aye, my dad uses them to measure his white powder at home.'

ULSTER ANSWERS TO 'WHY DID THE CHICKEN CROSS THE ROAD?'

SINN FEIN: That would be a matter for the chicken. Sinn Fein and the chicken are not part of the same organisation, although we share some ideals in common. If there are presently any chickens in Sinn Fein, we are not aware of it.

ORANGE ORDER: The chicken is entitled to walk in a peaceful manner on the Queen's Highway. It's a traditional route. Anyone who tries to deny the chicken his rights to walk on the road will find the road blocked at both ends until the chicken is allowed to walk in a dignified and non-threatening manner, with accompanying bands if need be.

IRA: On behalf of the people of Ireland, we reserve the right to defend the roads of the island against the chicken. For 800 years, the Irish people have resisted the imposition of chickens by force of arms and shall continue to do so until the chicken is expelled from our land. Anyone collaborating with the chicken, or assisting or enabling the imposition of road crossing by chickens, will be deemed legitimate targets in our struggle against tyranny.

UFF: We, the loyal defenders of Ulster roads, reserve our right to retaliate against any precipitate hostile actions by the chicken. We

 **TOM SHIELDS GOES FORTH**

shall meet force with deadly force. (A donation to the Loyalist Prisoners Association will ensure free passage of the chicken with respect to the road and the crossing thereof, till the same time next month anyhow. Do chickens have kneecaps?)

UUP/SDLP JOINT STATEMENT: We believe that only by working together in unison, and with the majority of the people of this island, the British and Irish Governments, and our friends overseas behind us, can we find the answer to this question. If we do not, or cannot, then our children will rightfully ask us the question, 'So why did the chicken cross the road?'

THE SECRETARY OF STATE FOR NORTHERN IRELAND: While not normally commenting on security matters, Her Majesty's Government feels it is right and proper, in this instance, to make a statement on this affair. Members of the Special Air Service involved in a covert anti-terrorist operation on the road at 8:42 this morning observed the chicken attempting to cross the road. As the chicken was approached by one of the soldiers involved, it was seen to make a threatening movement and action was taken to nullify that action. It has not yet been ascertained why the chicken was crossing the road, and it seems unlikely that we will now discover the motive.

20. AMERICAN POLITICS ARE A RUM AFFAIR

Tom Shields was sent to cover the Republican Convention 2000 in Philadelphia. He missed the point of the politics but learnt a few things about America.

The first question that must be asked about the Republican Party convention is why they are bothering holding it at all. Texan oil millionaire George Dubya Bush secured the Grand Old Party candidacy way back in March. His number two has been confirmed as Dick Cheney, another Texan oil millionaire. The huddled masses will be safe in their hands.

In the absence of any political business to be done here in Philadelphia, the assembly of 4,000 delegates, 15,000 members of the media, and numerous lobbyists and snake oil salespeople can get on with the serious business of partying. The system appears to be that major companies host a series of lavish bashes 'in honour' of some political figure. There is much drink and some musical entertainment. You can't get to them all but, on your behalf, I accepted the hospitality of the Chrysler car company, in honour of congressman J.C. Watts of Oklahoma. Music was by The

Temptations, an appropriate turn considering the potential for graft in the American political system. General Motors had Hank Williams Jr singing in honour of any GOP official anywhere in the United States. The American end of drinks company UDV honoured Californian republican David Dreier with a reception called the 'Dreier Martini'.

I couldn't fit in the salute to the House Republican leadership with Earth, Wind and Fire and, indeed, missed a concert in Philadelphia by Bob Dylan. Fear not, fellow '60s radicals, Bobby D wasn't singing for the Republicans. He just happened to be there, that's all.

As observers of political frolicking will know, convention partying can lead to frolicking, or houghmagandie as the Republicans do not call it. *The City* paper, part of the Philadelphia alternative press, offered a guide entitled: 'Where to find Bush and we don't mean the guy who wants to be president.' This guide to the many and exotic services on offer from the Philly sex industry was prefaced with the comment: 'Some Republicans are upright, straight-arrow teetotallers who don't smoke, swear, or cheat on their spouses. The rest of them are coming to Philadelphia . . .'

One of the many protest groups encamped in Philly is using as its slogan words about peace and justice by Gandhi, the great Indian peacemaker. The protesters will no doubt be desolate to know that the Mahatma's great-grandson is here as a Republican delegate. Shanti K. Gandhi is a heart surgeon from Topeka, Kansas. He recalls as a child the tumultuous scenes which surrounded his great-grandfather: 'We were always encountering big crowds. I didn't know what it was all about.' After studying medicine in Bombay, Gandhi came to Topeka, where he became involved in Republican politics. Yes, Gandhi Junior voted for Nixon.

The GOP is assiduous in wheeling out activists of ethnic origin: the Black Bush tendency, you might say. The multiracial types are still vastly outnumbered by the whites and rednecks who favour such Bush badges as 'Watch my lips. No new Texans.'

Running concurrently with the GOP convention is an exhibition called Politicalfest, which celebrates the joys of American politics.

The Politicalfest's main attraction is the replica of the White House oval office. Punters queue to have their photie taken sitting at the president's desk. Yes, your correspondent got in line. Yes, the nice lady in charge blushed gently when I asked the exact location of Bill Clinton's bit of hanky-panky with Monica. Yes, I had a cigar with me. Yes, it was Cuban. No, they didn't throw me out.

The Seagram drinks conglomerate is not content merely to lubricate the political process. It has put up its own presidential candidate. It is pushing Captain Morgan, of Spiced Rum fame, for president. Captain Morgan pledges to 'put the party back into politics'. His running mate (or rumming mate, as the Seagram PR people have it) is a former *Playboy* playmate by the name of Kalin Olsen.

I attended the Captain's reception. Not because of the presence of Ms Olsen, nor even because of the large selection of rum on offer (although the white spiced is particularly drinkable). It was an opportunity to talk to some Republicans in relaxed mood. But even in relaxed mood, they can be awfy po-faced. The Captain-Morgan-for-president ploy was all very well, said one, but it detracted from the serious business to be done in Philadelphia. This from a chap wearing a pair of breeks fashioned out of at least a dozen different tartans.

If the Republicans gathered here have a propensity to take themselves seriously, it is nothing compared to the earnestness of the many protest groups which have descended upon Philly. A rainbow alliance called Unity 2000 got together for a march on the eve of the convention. Among the issues bruited on the banners, according to the indispensable *National Journal* convention daily newspaper were poverty, injustice in the legal and prison systems, environmental degradation, racism, sexism, homophobia, religious intolerance, rapacious globalism, ever-growing militarism, declining support for education, and a political system which has been sold to the highest bidder. Also to the fore were protesters against the USA's crazy gun laws.

But there was one issue missing which appears to this correspondent to be crucial for the future of the American people. Philadelphia is officially the city with the fattest people in America.

This, as you will appreciate, is quite an achievement in the land of the porker. The blubber has to be seen to be believed. Never mind gun control – what this country needs is portion control.

The star of the Republican convention so far is Colin Powell, the black military man turned politician. There is a question I have been anxious to ask Mr Powell: how come his first name is pronounced Coalin? Does he have any Ayrshire roots? Or is he named after some speaker of broad Scots who emigrated to America? I very nearly got to ask Coalin, since he was only yards away from me.

Unfortunately, he was at a reception inside the Striped Bass, a swish Philadelphia restaurant, and I was outside. Outside trying to get in, with no success. A hard-nosed lady was on the door. She was sympathetic, but unswayed by the information that failure to get a story from this gig would lead to my instant dismissal. Where would I get another job at my age? I would not be able to send my children to college. Was not the Republican slogan this year 'Leave no child behind'?

When it became obvious that no amount of reasoned argument would secure admission to these convention events, the next best thing was to test that famous Republican sense of humour. But the line 'Donald Dewar wants me to pass on fraternal greetings' always goes right over their heads.

Having come to terms with my failure to meet the powerful and famous, I took refuge at the round bar in the foyer of the Marriott Hotel, where I met with rejection yet again, as the barmaid said she was busy replenishing stock and could serve me, possibly, in half an hour. Then this amazingly suave and good-looking black guy sat down on the next bar stool. He gave the barmaid a beaming smile and a warm greeting. Within seconds, he had a glass of brandy in front of him and was enjoying a huge cigar. There was then a procession of people asking to shake his hand and telling him how much they loved his movies.

The chap, it transpires, was Richard Roundtree of *Shaft* fame, in town to lend his support to the Republican cause. He thinks the remake of the *Shaft* movie could have been better. He hates the word nigger, even when used in context. Well, you can't help overhearing sometimes.

The Black Bush tendency grows apace. The Grand Old Party is going full out to show it is no longer merely the redoubt of the wealthy, white male – their membership includes millionaires regardless of race, gender, or sexual orientation. The chairman of the National Black Republican Committee was put up to speak as an example. Fred Brown spoke volumes when he said that 'the only colour of freedom is green'. That's greenbacks, not green politics.

On a slow news day at the convention, even this correspondent was interviewed by Philly TV. They did not seek to benefit from my political insight. They wanted to hear of my experiences in the hotel from hell. Due to leaving the booking too late, and the tight budget available for the excursion, your reporter was billeted in a hotel which can best be described as modest. The word grubby also springs to mind.

When I booked in early on Sunday morning, there was much toing and froing of loud and lively young people. Imagine a whole bunch of people who had just been on the *Jerry Springer* show getting together for a party, and you have the scene.

The next day, the partying had given way to religion as the hotel's banqueting rooms played host to gospel services by the likes of the Church of the Power of the Name. The hotel has many banqueting rooms, but does not offer guests any food or drink.

Your reporter was enduring rather than enjoying his stay when it was abruptly ended at 3.30 a.m. by a pounding at the bedroom door. It was a fireman in breathing apparatus, indicating that a hasty exit from the hotel was in order. There was a gas leak and the basement was filled with carbon monoxide.

So there I was, standing in the parking lot in torrential rain. We'd been told that the Red Cross had been informed of our homeless predicament. A passing Philadelphia polis asked, in the cheerful way they have been told to adopt with visitors: 'Hi! How ya doin'?' I told him how I was doing. Exactly how I was doing.

Now, I wonder, what's the Republican policy on homeless Scottish refugees?

In their new, caring, inclusive way, the Republican Party is working its way through the minorities. Latest in the list was American war heroes, stirring stuff and much more fun than being nice to the

coloured folk, a process that has occupied much of the convention this week. The tribute to the Second World War generation was a perfect excuse to play 'Anchors Aweigh' and other strident music, and to show film clips of GI Joe in action.

It was all a bit like the end scenes in those movies where the Yanks won the war.

Stormin' Norman Schwarzkopf addressed the nation from the decks of the battleship USS *New Jersey*. The ship was actually parked only a few miles from the convention venue in Philadelphia, and Stormin' could easily have called in personally, but let's not spoil the effect.

There were a few Republican war heroes present. Senator Bob Dole is the genuine article, severely wounded saving a comrade's life in Italy in 1945. Then there was Bush Snr, who had seen plenty of action. John McCain, himself a veteran of the Vietnam conflict, recalled that his grandfather, a four-star admiral, had been George Bush's commanding officer. That's Bush Snr. Bush Jnr was also a military man. At the time of the Vietnam war, George Dubya was a pilot of F102 jet fighters. He was attached to the Texas militia air force. I don't know much about militia matters, but this sounds a bit like being a submarine commander with Strathclyde polis. Anyway, while the fighting was going on over there, Dubya was making sure the skies over Texas were safe.

M uch was also made of the fact that an unashamed, out-of-the-closet gay congressman was to speak at the convention. Congressman Jim Kolbe spoke about trade. Free trade, not rough trade. He spoke about protectionism, of the commercial and not the safe-sex variety. There were fears of discordant protests from the redneck contingency, but the worst that happened was the Texan delegates refusing to take off their cowboy hats.

There was a chap at the convention who might have made a stronger protest. He is Pat Robertson, of the gay-bashing evangelist and Bank of Scotland tendency. But, like most of the Republican loonies, Pat Robertson had been locked away for the duration. When he managed to escape from the attic long enough to appear on TV, even Pat appeared moderate. He said he could not endorse Mr Kolbe's lifestyle, but added that he 'encouraged gay men to succeed'. A soundbite that could be misinterpreted by anyone who knows the old joke about budgies and seed.

The USA is a diverse and colourful nation, but that does not begin to explain some of the exotic names which cropped up. A woman called Ave Maria Bie. A man called Dick Posthumus. And a woman, one of Dubya's close advisers, who glories in the first name Condoleezza. Not for nothing does the second amendment of the constitution give citizens the inalienable right to have bizarre monickers.

A schmoozing session (sorry, this political stuff is catching) between Republicans and the International Brotherhood of Teamsters gave an opportunity to watch James Hoffa in action. Son of the legendary union boss, James Jnr is a reformer and the Mr Clean of modern American trade unionism. So why did Mr Hoffa and so many of his colleagues remind me of Rod Steiger in *On the Waterfront*? I had an urge, ill-advised and possibly life-threatening, to approach a sharp-suited Teamster and say: 'Charlie, I could have been a contender.'

Instead, I asked: 'Are you guys Teamsters?' 'No, we're girl scouts,' came the reply. 'You're Scottish,' said Joe from New Jersey, adding: 'It's a short swim to Belfast.' Spotting a certain nervousness on the part of your reporter, Joe explained that he had friends in Belfast. Joe then insisted that I help myself to a drink and some shrimp from the buffet. You wouldn't want to argue with these American girl scouts.

The protesters on the streets of Philly are mainly of the left-wing persuasion, so a bunch of people in favour of the death penalty thought they would balance the scales. They were wearing T-shirts saying 'Kill Mumia'. Mumia Abu-Jamal is on death row after being convicted of killing a Philadelphia policeman. The fans of the electric chair chose as the gathering point for their protest Geno's, a famous city steakhouse. A location ideal for bloody or well-done metaphors? You bet. 'Let him fry!' was one of the placards.

The feared violent confrontation between protesters and police at the Philadelphia Republican convention did not come to pass. Attempts by hardline dissidents to provoke the police were met with restraint, and the policy of arresting and locking up ringleaders has also helped the police cause. There was a surreal quality to the cat-and-mouse game going on in the streets. '100 anarchists in clown suits blocking Broad Street' is not the kind of alert a Philly cop usually has to respond to.

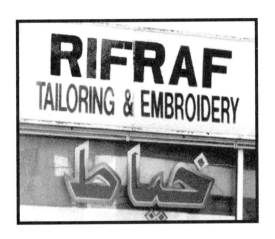

The battles of the bikes are something of an improvement on more lurid moments in the Philadelphia police department's history, such as the Thomas Jones case, when a captured carjacker was beaten to a pulp live on the TV evening news. Or their crowning glory in 1985, when their method of dealing with a bunch of radicals holed up in a building was to drop a suitcase of explosives from a police helicopter. The explosion killed 11 people, including five children, and the subsequent fire destroyed a whole city block.

With not a lot to do at the four-day convention, the Republicans filled many happy hours with the roll call. This is the bit where each delegation declares its votes. The declaration is usually preceded by a lengthy and bombastic description of the state, a list of name checks, and an unashamed plug for local industry and commerce. The speaker will proudly say that their state is the world leader in succotash, or kumquat-growing, or that the new Republican administration has reduced the incidence of brothers marrying sisters by more than 50 per cent.

Some of the states made quite modest claims that week: the lady from Utah said theirs was the only state beginning with U; the man from Nebraska was proud to say that his was the only state never to have been visited by Bill Clinton since he became president; and the smooth-talking representative of Tennessee made his home state sound appealing. 'Tennessee,' he said, 'home of beautiful women and fast horses . . .'

Continuing the trip around the ethnic groups at this convention, I caught up with the Irish Republicans. No, there was no sign of Gerry Adams, Martin McGuinness or any of the other boys from the old brigade.

There was a reception, an outdoor party, called the IRA Palooza. It turned out not to be canapes and cocktails with the military wing of the Sinn Fein, but a get-together sponsored by various financial corporations to promote IRA legislation. That's Individual Retirement Accounts.

The official, proper Irish Republicans offered hospitality at their Blarney Bash. This consisted of lashings of seafood, oceans of Guinness, and earfuls of Irish songs. You could not miss the host,

Frank Duggan of the Irish Republicans committee. He was six-foot-something and wearing a green leprechaun hat.

Weren't most Irish Americans Democrats? I asked.

Frank replied: 'I'm a former Democrat, a recovering Democrat.' Frank defected to the Republicans after a leading Democrat made a tasteless joke in public about the Pope. (No, Frank wouldn't tell me the joke.)

The GOP is perceived as pretty much a WASP institution. This was not helped by George Dubya's recent tacit endorsement of Bob Jones University, spiritual home of extreme Protestantism. The Republicans attempted to woo the Catholic Church with a special box at the First Union Center sports complex, where the convention was being held. I have never seen so many clerics at a sporting venue since the days when Celtic used to let the priests in for free.

Yet another ethnic minority was present, this time a minority of one – Gary Nakamoto, a computer company vice-president from McLean, Virginia, a Japanese-Scottish Republican. His Caledonian roots, and a hint of Scots twang, come from his mother, Janet McPherson. Another defected Democrat, Gary says he gets more respect from the Republicans.

With the intense security surrounding the convention site, having to pass through the metal-detecting doors was a regular occurrence. One lady delegate kept sending off the alarm signals. The problem was that she had so many commemorative campaign buttons, badges, and pins attached to her jacket. The security people asked her to remove the garment. She duly did, revealing that she wore nothing underneath. An embarrassed steward apologised as the lady walked topless through security. The lady was unfazed, declaring that she was a nudist. Yet another Republican minority.

If you miss one Bush at the Republican convention in Philadelphia, don't worry. There will another one along in a minute. On nomination night, George Dubya was the last Bush to turn up.

Earlier, brother Jeb, in his capacity as governor of Florida, cast that state's votes in favour of his sibling. Jeb shared with the nation how big brother used to give him a 'wedgie'. Dubya would pick him

up by the Y-fronts, which garment would become firmly wedged... You get the picture.

George P (for Prescott) is an ace in his uncle's campaign. A sexy Latino twenty-something, he appeals to the young Hispanic vote and to females of all ages. He is also earnest and active and a future Bush president in waiting.

There is, unfortunately, another nephew, called Pierce Bush. He is a precocious child who comes on TV and utters through his braced teeth such platitudes as 'my uncle will restore dignity to the White House'. He is a politician in miniature and regularly interrupts conversation at the Bush dinner table to ask how such and such a policy might affect the economy. A swift kick up the Pokemon would not go amiss.

George Dubya admits he is not the sharpest tool in the box. He is living proof that a pupil who gets straight Cs at school can still aspire to be president. In a college English paper, young Dubya was asked to illustrate a synonym for the word tears. He wrote: 'Lacerates ran down my cheek.'

A lack of learning may not be a bad thing in a president. Care and compassion are better qualities. George Dubya claims to be a compassionate conservative. In his acceptance speech he spoke with sadness about meeting teenage boys who had committed adult crimes and were going down a hard road.

The same George W, as governor of Texas, has signed the death warrants of 127 prisoners since he took office. That is one execution every fortnight. The same George W speaks of his gubernatorial efficiency which has reduced from 30 to 15 minutes the time it takes to review each death row case.

The city of Philadelphia gave a little goodie bag to each of the 15,000 journalists here to cover the Republican convention. As well as maps and glossy brochures, the bag contained a box of Kraft elephant-shaped macaroni and a self-help booklet.

I am keeping the macaroni in reserve, in case there is a sudden food shortage in the USA. The booklet has already been pressed into use. It is based on the works of the late Dale Carnegie, of *How to Win Friends and Influence People* fame. Mr Carnegie's precepts really can help you through an average day in the midst of the Republicans,

like: 'Fill your mind with thoughts of peace, courage, health and hope.' And: 'Remember that a person's name is to that person the sweetest and most important sound in any language.' These do seem to work. But another of the Carnegie hints on becoming a friendlier person is harder to master. It is: 'Arouse in the other person an eager want.'

21. WHEN JOHN PAUL MET FIDEL

26 JANUARY 1998

It all started to go wrong when the Vatican told me there was no room on the Pope's plane. Obviously Cardinal Tom Winning's influence with the Pontiff is on the wane, not to mention that of Father Tom Connelly of the Scottish Catholic Press Office.

Then my application for accreditation for the papal visit, already two weeks late, got lost somewhere between Glasgow, London and Havana. But the flight was booked and paid for, so the trip to witness the encounter between Fidel Castro and John Paul II, the world's most charismatic leaders (probably the *only* charismatic heads of state left in the world today), was definitely on.

The accreditation problem could be sorted out in Havana. But I had not counted on the inflexibility of the Cuban Communist's bureaucratic system. The man from the Ministry in the international press centre in Havana was friendly but firm. No accreditation – and, since I was in Cuba on a tourist visa, I could not work as a journalist. But surely, I argued, the most important aspect of the Pope's visit was to show what a progressive and democratic country

Cuba is. The man from the Ministry hinted that, with all the world's TV networks and news agencies among the 3,000 media people already accredited, they could probably get by without the help of the *Herald*. 'My friend,' he said, 'for your stay in Cuba you are not a reporter, you are a pilgrim. It would not be advisable for you to go around saying you are a journalist. Do not interview people and do not send stories back while you are here or we may have to come and talk to you.'

So what you are reading is not a report on the papal visit to Cuba. It is a rather lengthy postcard from an accidental pilgrim.

It was a pilgrimage to see not only the Pope but also Fidel, who is a legendary figure to us ageing '60s radicals. We are all getting older, but the first sighting of Fidel was something of a shock. It was on TV – as close, in fact, as most of the 3,000 press got to the man. Castro had decided to address the nation on the subjects of the recent elections to the Cuban Parliament and the Pope's visit. He spoke for six hours. Or rather, he was on screen for six hours. Ever the man for a long speech, he is now taking matters to excess. At 71, he is showing signs of wear and tear. There were long pauses when

he seemed to have forgotten what he wanted to say. Then he would search through the sheaves of paper in front of him. Some of the pauses were so long you could pop out and make a cup of tea and not miss much.

Despite the length of the speech, Castro's message was quite short. The Cuban revolution is in good nick. The capitalist system is in crisis, the Cuban voters had shown great common sense by voting him and his comrades back into power. And everyone was to turn out to see the Pope and 'utter not one word of protest or disrespect'.

For those who missed the six-hour speech, there was a repeat on the Sunday. For those who missed the repeat, the speech was extensively reported in the state daily newspaper *Granma*, occupying five of its 12 pages. This was three pages fewer than the report of his previous pre-election speech, in which he covered every subject under the sun and concluded with the words 'and that's all I've got to say on the matter'.

Fidel's stuff in *Granma* may be long-winded, but it's still a much better read than the rest of its content – unless you are really interested in the heroic struggle of the cane-cutting brigades to bring in the sugar harvest, or the sterling efforts of the meter readers at the Cuban Electricity Board. For light relief there is *Radio Reloj*, the Clock Radio, a station which consists of continuous news items read out to the background noise of a ticking clock with pips and a timecheck every minute. It is a great cure for insomnia.

But back to the Pope. Not being invited to join the platform party at Jose Marti's airport, I watched his arrival on TV in the bar of the Hotel Colina in the company of some exuberant Colombian fellow pilgrims. The Colombians were being shepherded energetically by a monk in a green habit with a very smart leather John Lennon cap, who made even more noise than his flock.

To greet the Pope, Fidel discarded his scruffy army fatigues and was wearing a nice suit that would have made his mother, Lina, proud. His mum was forever praying and lighting candles in the church she attended, or so we are told in the book *Fidel and Religion* which has been selling at inflated prices in Havana's second-hand book stalls to journalists in search of a spot of plagiarism. The book explains much about Fidel's attitude, including a hint as to why he banned Christmas when he got into power. In it, he relates that as a young

Head of policy

IT was stated yesterday that Neil Greig is head of policy for Alcoholics Anonymous. Mr Greig is in fact head of policy for the Automobile Association (AA).

boy, for three years in a row, he got a trumpet for Christmas – a slightly different trumpet each year, but another trumpet all the same.

He also says that his Jesuit education left him unconvinced about religion, but instilled in him two qualities which stood him in good stead as a guerrilla leader: he developed the ability to make very long speeches and, having joined the school scout troop, spent a lot of time in the mountains of Cuba practising survival techniques.

His school report from the Jesuits was prophetic; 'Fidel will fill the book of his life with brilliant pages. He is made of strong wood.'

Meanwhile, back at the airport, Fidel kept his speech down to 11 minutes. He still managed to fit in references to the Spanish Inquisition, Galileo, the Crusades and the murder of 70 million Indians by the Conquistadores. At least, I was sure that's what Fidel said, or as sure as I could be over the noise of the Colombians. A Cuban chap beside me decided to complicate matters further by giving me a translation in broken English. After the Pope's speech, the Cuban was visibly moved. He said: 'With the arrival of El Papa we are breathing a new air in Cuba (slight pause). Would you like to come back to my house? I have lobster, Havana club rum, CocaCola and cigars. Twenty dollars.' Most conversations with Cubans begin or end with an offer to provide goods or services in return for dollars. (The Cuban microeconomy is a complex and fascinating subject, to which I hope to return in a future article.)

Not being invited by either Fidel or JP II to pop round for supper and a chat, I headed on a pilgrim's tour of Old Havana. The bullet holes are still there, preserved as a monument on the building in the main square where cronies of the dictator Batista were holding out against Castro's rebel band. A quick rake of machine gun fire changed their minds.

Another monument worth visiting is the Castillo de Farnes, a restaurant where Fidel and Che Guevara turned up at 3.45 a.m. one morning shortly after Havana was taken. There are some evocative photographs of the two bearded ones who, having had a busy day at the revolution, were in need of some sustenance and a cigar or two.

The Castillo de Farnes is still much the same as it was in 1959, if you don't count the video jukebox and the lycra-clad lovelies on the hunt for dollars. This place of homage to the revolution has the advantage of selling half-decent Spanish-style food and extremely decent Rioja.

Back on the papal trail, the Holy Father's first mass was held in Santa Clara, a town some 200 miles from Havana. The American TV networks had hired all the really flash and comfortable transport, but there was still a car and driver available from the state taxi company at $500 for the round trip. I managed to get a much cheaper quote of $200 from a young man called Enrique, who was in the process of setting himself up in the tourism industry on a freelance basis. The only other way would have been to travel by *gua-gua* (pronounced wah-wah), as the Cubans call their buses. But services are few and far between, and as my Havana advisers told me, booking a ticket would be only marginally less complex than getting my accreditation for the Papal visit.

So at 4 a.m., there I was in Enrique's Lada heading out of Havana. The pitch-black night made it difficult to spot the ubiquitous potholes, but had the benefit of concealing the extent of the decrepitude of Enrique's vehicle. The clattering noises, the smell of petrol, the occasional cough of the engine and the dim headlights were clues enough. But Enrique was much better company than, forinstance, those TV and news agency people flashing past in their smart people carriers with such things as air conditioning and seatbelts.

As dawn broke, I could see that the rear view mirror of the ageing Lada was adorned with a pair of fluffy dice in a state of severe deterioration. I contemplated telling Enrique that this was not the kind of image for a young man starting out in the tourist courier trade, but couldn't remember the Spanish for fluffy dice. (Yes, I know now, it's *dados vellosos*.)

Santa Clara is a long way to go for a Mass, but looks quite enchanting as the mist lifts over the orange groves and the sugar fields. The morning star is low in the sky ahead, which seems entirely appropriate for a journey in this Communist country. Santa Clara is the smallest and least scenic of the four cities where the Papal Masses are being held. The venue is a scruffy field, the sports ground of a local gym college. The altar is a huge wooden structure roofed with palm leaves and looks like a beachside bar at a Club Med resort. An earnest young man asks if I am with the New York pilgrims. He doesn't understand when I reply that I'm with the Scottish Tims.

Up on the big garden hut of an altar, a wee nun is leading the singing to keep us occupied until the Pope arrives. Cuba, a land

renowned for its rhythm and song, has managed to choose a nun with a strident and tuneless voice as the Pope's warm-up act. Even more painful than the ear-bashing from The Little Sister of Discordancy is the baking sun which is turning my forehead a deep lobster pink, to the consternation of the three Cuban matrons standing beside me. A lady nearby is suffering a fainting spell and, much to the confusion of the Red Cross attendants, she keeps recovering and refuses to be stretchered away from the scene.

The Pope arrives and, courtesy of a pair of binoculars borrowed from one of the Cuban ladies, I can see he is suffering nearly as much as I am from the heat. JP II's theme for the day is the importance of family life, to which I can relate, having been adopted by the Cuban ladies. They have even got me singing from their hymn sheet.

Two hours later, and with an hour of the ceremonies still to go, I am forced to retreat to the shade. By a stroke of luck, I chance upon a rarity in these parts; a cafeteria catering for tourists in the centre of Santa Clara. It has a full range of cooling drinks, including Spanish Cava. However, visions of a glass of chilled sparkling wine are dashed when the barman informs me that, out of respect to His Holiness, there will be no alcoholic drinks consumed while the Pope is saying Mass.

Back on the revolutionary trail, we discover that Santa Clara played a crucial role in the overthrow of the Batista regime. The town is littered with memorials to Che Guevara, who led the rebels to a famous victory here. Like the elegant building in Havana, the facade of the Santa Clara Libre Hotel also has battle scars in the form of bullet holes, but unlike its comrade, this concrete monstrosity has actually been improved by leaving the damage unrepaired. Another cheery memorial is a derailed armoured train left by the trackside, alongside the bulldozer which Che's men used to halt its progress.

Santa Clara is also the home to the Che Guevara mausoleum, where the revolutionary hero's remains are kept. It should be very moving, except for the odd stray thought that so few of Che's bones were recovered from the Bolivian jungle that they fit into a wooden box so small that it looks more like a cigar humidor than a coffin.

Whatever Santa Clara did for the Cuban revolution, the revolution appears to have done little for Santa Clara and its people. Horse-drawn trams are a testament to the ongoing fuel crisis. Doleful and down-at-heel citizens queue to be allowed into a drab cafe, so different from the smart tourist bar, to spend their pesos on meagre fare.